SPaG BOOK

A Teacher's Guide to Spelling, Punctuation, and Grammar

MATILDA ROSE

Edited by M J BROMLEY

autus
books

AUTUS BOOKS
England, UK

First published in 2013

ISBN-13: 978-1484113493
ISBN-10: 1484113497

For my sisters

Contents

Chapter 1
Introduction

Grammar has been in and out of style more times than flared trousers but now the fickle pendulum of fashion has swung once more in its favour. So sing it from the rooftops: spelling, punctuation, and grammar are en vogue! Yes, SPaG is sexy!

Throughout the first half of the twentieth century, grammar was a fashion icon, invited to all the best parties and oft seen flaunting herself at red carpet events, dancing in a shimmer of paparazzi flashlight. But times change and soon grammar became an embarrassment, a remnant of a bygone age. By 1960, she couldn't get a table at The Ivy for love nor money. Instead, she vanished from public gaze, regarded as passé, hidden at the back of a wardrobe, there to remain throughout the 1960s, '70s and '80s.

Her moth-eaten remains were finally dragged off the hanger and into the light in the 1990s. But, despite a impassioned comeback under the guise of the National Literacy Strategy, grammar remained marginalised, imprisoned behind the electrified fence of English lessons.

She was back but still much maligned and misunderstood.

Until now.

Now, having pulled off a daring escape, grammar is back with a vengeance. She has scaled the prison walls of English lessons to become an integral part of the whole school curriculum in primary and secondary schools in England. She's resurrected, renewed: rejoice!

*

PART ONE

SPaG in theory

"It's impossible to teach grammar for the simple reason that no one knows what it is..."

Chapter 2
SPaG: A brief history

Once upon a time, SPaG was king of the world.

Before 1960, grammar was the most important subject on the school timetable - so important in fact that some schools were even called 'grammar schools'. Its pedigree stretches back much further than this, though. In the ancient world, grammar teaching was highly regarded as a means of developing students' writing skills (the word 'grammar', after all, comes from the Greek letter gamma which was the 'written character') as well as a means of developing students' thinking skills. In the eighteenth century, however, grammar teaching began to wither on the vine.

By 1800 grammar teaching had been largely reduced to a set of strict rules designed to help students avoid grammatical errors. In the nineteenth century, English literature established itself as a university subject, competing with grammar (or English language as it had become known) for supremacy. Over time, following an energetic campaign, English literature won the battle (and was crowned 'English') and was presented as a liberal and liberating alternative to English language and the so-called 'grammar-grind'.

In the first half of the twentieth century, although grammar was still taught (and indeed was still highly regarded), there was a steady decline in the quality of grammar teaching in English schools, and increasing calls for its abolishment. One reason for this decline was the complete lack of university-level research on English grammar, which led a government report in 1921 to conclude that it was "...impossible at the present juncture to teach English grammar in schools for the simple reason that no one knows exactly what it is...".

In the latter half of the twentieth century, starting in 1960, the majority of schools stopped teaching grammar in English lessons. By cruel coincidence, grammar stopped being taught as part of MFL lessons and the teaching of Latin died out in most state schools. These three factors led to a situation whereby students no longer had any access to a systematic instruction in grammar.

At the end of the twentieth century, however, things began to change. The Bullock Report of 1975 signalled a reversal of grammar's fortunes. Bullock was followed by several other government reports - supported by a blossoming bed of university linguistics departments[1] - which argued that English teaching was failing in its main aim to teach literacy. But rather than calling for a reintroduction of traditional grammar teaching in schools, these reports suggested that traditional grammar teaching should be replaced by a new 'tools not rules' model.

And so, as a new millennium dawned, the National Literacy Strategy was born. It was grammar but not as we knew it...

---

[1] Paradoxically, whilst grammar lay bleeding on the gym floor of English schools, it once again became an important research subject at university, partly driven by the publishing market in Teaching English as a Foreign Language (TEFL). Before long, most universities had a department of linguistics or of English language where undergraduates studied grammar.

Chapter 3
What is SPaG?

SPaG stands for 'spelling, punctuation, and grammar'. I'm going to make an ass out of you and me and *assume* you already know what is meant by the word 'spelling' and also by the word 'punctuation'[2]. But 'grammar'? That's a little trickier, isn't it? If you can't quite put your hands on a satisfactory definition of that elusive concept 'grammar', then relax: you're not alone. Even linguistics experts have difficulty agreeing on what grammar means in practice...

A QCA document published in 1998 called 'The Grammar Papers' dedicates six full pages to defining 'grammar'. Luckily for you, I've read it so you don't have to! Put simply, the QCA paper suggests that grammar "includes syntax, morphology and semantics and was originally

[2] If you're in any doubt, keep reading... *Part Two* has everything you need to know about spelling and punctuation.

associated with logic and rhetoric." The most important conclusion to draw from this definition is this: grammar is not just syntax, as many people believe. Instead, that word 'grammar' includes all of the following elements:

- **Syntax**: the study of sentence structure, an analysis of main and subordinate clauses, of simple, compound and complex sentences, of subjects, verbs and objects, and so on;

- **Morphology**: the study of word structure, an analysis of stem (or root) words, of prefixes and suffixes, inflections for tense, number and person, and so on;

- **Semantics**: the study of meaning, an analysis of the things, people, and events we refer to when we're talking, as well as how meanings - both literal (denotation) and implied (connotation) - are conveyed, and how words can mask their true meaning (e.g. through the use of euphemism)[3].

So that's syntax, morphology and semantics taken care of... but what about logic and rhetoric..?

Traditionally, grammar was associated with logic and rhetoric because it was thought that a grammatical pattern such as a choice of tense could make a major

---

[3] If any of this sounds likes a foreign language to you, then never fear: all will be explained in *Part Two* of this book.

difference to the logical and communicative effect of a sentence. In short, it was thought that grammar teaching should be as concerned with the 'effects' of grammatical structures as with these structures themselves.

The great rhetoricians like Aristotle first recognised the interconnectedness of language and thought. Aristotle phrased this as the difference between *logos* (the logical content of a speech) and *lexis* (the style and delivery of a speech). Roman authors such as Quintilian made the same distinction by dividing the consideration of things or substance, *res*, from the consideration of verbal expression, *verba*.

Rhetoricians divided form and content like this not to place content above form but to highlight the interdependence of language and meaning – to suggest that how you say something and what you say are dependent on each other: this means that what you say can be enhanced or depreciated by the language you use to say it. In other words, grammar is not merely instrumental; it is fundamental. The way we use grammatical features is fundamental not only to communication but to thought itself because our language choices directly influence how people think and feel.

So that's how 'The Grammar Pages' defines 'grammar'. Let's take a quick look at two other definitions....

The National Curriculum and the National Literacy

Strategy define grammar as including the following:

- Vocabulary and 'word families';

-Sound patterns in words and the phoneme-grapheme[4] correspondences of phonics;

- Intonation in speech and its effects on meaning.

According to the Key Stage 3 programmes of study in English, grammar is concerned with a study of language at:

- Word level, which includes morphology[5];

- Sentence level, which includes syntax[6];

- Text level, which involves semantics[7] and rhetorical effects.

What aspects of SPaG should be taught in

[4] A phoneme is a unit of sound; a grapheme is a unit of writing. Phoneme-grapheme is about the connectedness (or indeed separateness) between the way a word is written and the way it sounds when spoken. Many English words are not spelt phonetically because they derive from a foreign language. More on this in *Part Two*.

[5] Morphology: how words are made. More in *Part Two*.

[6] As we have seen, syntax is the study of sentence structure.

[7] As we have seen, semantics is the study of meaning.

schools?

Whatever definition of grammar we settle for, it's clear it must include the linguistic structures of <u>words</u>, <u>sentences</u> and whole <u>texts</u>. In order to ensure that grammar is taught effectively, therefore, children must be taught:

- the word classes (or parts of speech) and their grammatical functions;

- the structure of phrases and clauses and how they can be combined (by coordination and subordination) to make complex sentences;

- paragraph structure and how to form different types of paragraph;

- the structure of whole texts, including cohesion, and the conventions of openings and conclusions in different types of writing; and

- the use of appropriate grammatical terminology in order to reflect on the meaning and clarity of both spoken and written language.

Is that all? What else should children be taught? Here's a few suggestions to get us started...

Children need to be taught to use grammatical terminology and to use grammatical knowledge when reading and writing. For example, children need to be taught the organising principles and structures of language and how they contribute to meaning and effect. At its simplest, children should be taught how grammatical features can be used to affect meaning. For example, "a small cup" is an adjective + a common noun and the adjective modifies the meaning of the common noun.

Children should also be taught to recognise standard features of English and to refer to uses of English which do not conform to this standard as either 'non-standard' or 'dialectal variations' rather than to see them as mistakes. For example, the use of the double negative "I didn't do nothing" is not wrong; it is a feature of many British dialects and conforms to a set of conventions every bit as much as the standard English "I didn't do anything". Other features of non-standard English or dialectal variation which should be taught are subject-verb agreement, the formation of past tense, adverbs and negatives, and the use of pronouns and prepositions[8].

Distinguishing between standard and non-standard (rather than right and wrong) in this way is what's called a *descriptive* - rather than a *prescriptive* - approach to grammar. In teaching grammar, we should not prescribe

[8] It's worth remembering that a child who speaks a non-standard dialect has to learn a new set of grammar rules in order to be able to use standard English in their writing. It therefore makes sense to address these grammatical differences directly as part of our grammar teaching and to present them as differences rather than mistakes.

what children should say nor should we proscribe what they should not say. Often, the grammar teaching of old was based on false premises. For example, we used to teach children that splitting an infinitive (as in, 'to boldly go') was wrong simply because it is not possible to split an infinitive in Latin. But English is not Latin. There is no reason why splitting an infinitive should be 'wrong' in English. Today, thankfully, grammar teaching is much less dogmatic.

The National Literacy Strategy called this new pragmatic approach 'tools not rules'.

Children, in the latter stages of their education, should also be helped to connect their grammatical knowledge to a wider knowledge of how language changes over time and place, and how language is learned. At A Level, for example, students of English language study the processes of child language acquisition, as well as language change, and this knowledge invariably helps them to understand English grammar better.

Chapter 4
Why do we need to teach SPaG?

We now understand what 'grammar' actually is (or at least we understand it as well as anyone else) and have some ideas about what aspects of grammar we need to teach in schools... but why? Why is it important that we teach grammar in schools at all? After all, as we've already learnt, grammar wasn't taught in state schools for the best part of thirty years. Well...

According to the National Literacy Strategy, the only explicit justification for teaching grammar is its contribution to writing skills. Grammar teaching, the theory goes, promotes students' understanding and helps them to know, notice, discuss and explore language features. The quality of students' writing is also affected by their motivation, creativity and insight, all of which may also be improved by grammar teaching. Grammar teaching may also provide a tool for learning other languages.

But does it work? Does grammar teaching really lead to improved writing?

There is a great deal of solid research evidence *against* the claim that grammar teaching improves writing. But wherever grammar teaching has been proven to have a positive effect on writing, it is always because:

- grammar teaching is integrated into the curriculum, not a stand-alone 'grammar lesson';

- grammar teaching has a well-defined focus (it is a means to an end);

- grammar teaching is well-planned to ensure development over time (or 'grammar growth');

- grammatical features of texts are related to their function, effect and meaning (i.e. grammatical features are placed in context not studied in cold isolation).

Let's return to my earlier claim that "grammar teaching promotes students' understanding and helps them to *know, notice, discuss and explore language features*". Richard Hudson, a retired professor of linguistics at University College London, and one of the founding fathers of the National Literacy Strategy, says that "the solution [to improving students' writing is grammar] teaching which is sufficiently explicit about the language of writing [in order] to promote five effects in children, each of which has major implications for how grammar is taught". Hudson sets out these five effects as follows:

Understanding - pupils should understand how language 'works' - how it is organised, how sentences are organised and how they are used to achieve particular effects. All these goals are included in the National Curriculum under the heading 'knowledge, skills and understanding'. This target requires clarity and consistency in the teaching, and constant revisiting of ideas in order to highlight connections.

Knowing - "Pupils are expected to be familiar with the grammatical terms and concepts relating to word, sentence and whole text structure that are outlined in the English programmes of study."[9] This means that the teaching must give children whatever detailed knowledge is required to cope with the 'technicalities' of the grammatical analysis which you think is suitable for their age and ability. For teaching methods this suggests practice and discussion where technical language is expected. And of course, pupils may come to know a few new grammatical patterns through direct instruction, even though they must learn most of them through experience.

Noticing - pupils should pay attention to grammatical features: "An essential element in 'the routine discussion' and teaching about language is 'noticing'. It is a modest word unsupported but also unencumbered by educational theory yet it aptly describes a way in which much

---

[9] Here, Hudson quotes 'The Grammar Papers'.

learning about language - spelling, vocabulary, punctuation, grammar - is actually accomplished. Accumulated noticing accounts for a considerable amount of language knowledge and proficiency."[10] For example, asking pupils to look at the way pronouns are used in a particular text makes them notice the pronouns in a way that they would not otherwise do, and increases the chances that they will learn something about pronouns from reading that text. Here the implication for teaching is that grammar should be applied to texts.

Discussing - teachers should encourage "discussion - to shape and challenge developing ideas"[11]. This implies that pupils should be able to talk about grammatical patterns (using technical terminology), but also that they should be able to defend ideas and analyses rather than simply regurgitate facts. If discussion is managed well it leads to a deeper understanding of the ideas concerned, and might involve either the whole class or groups.

Investigating - "Effective grammar teaching should encourage pupil investigation"[12] and the literacy strategy already encourages "investigations - in which pupils explore language and work out its rules and conventions"[13]. Small-scale investigations are particularly suitable as starter-activities; for example, the class might:

---

[10] Hudson is quoting 'Not Whether But How' published by the QCA in 1999.

[11] Hudson is quoting the KS3 Framework for English.

[12] From 'The Grammar Papers'.

[13] The KS3 Framework.

- investigate the 'family' of words related to some target word by dividing into teams and competing to find the most words;
- look for alternative meanings in a phrase such as "more intelligent pupils like us";
- compare standard and non-standard past-tense verb forms.

The combined effect of these five activities, Hudson concludes, "should be faster and more confident grammar growth".

And as for my other claim that "the quality of students' writing is also affected by their *motivation, creativity and insight*, all of which may also be improved by grammar teaching", here's Hudson again, who says that students write better if they have:

- **Motivation** to write well, e.g. if [they] badly want to impress or to be understood.
- **Creativity** - i.e. if [they] can think of interesting things to say and original ways of saying them.
- **Insight** - i.e. if [they] have a clear understanding of what kind of writing the teacher wants.

The student 'activities' generated by grammar teaching are also relevant to these components of writing. For example:

Motivation - discussion and investigation increase motivation, as when a writing task follows a grammar exploration which was fun or interesting.

Creativity - noticing an original use of language is a good step towards creativity in one's own performance, especially if reinforced by discussion and investigation. Indeed, the more grammar we have, and the better we understand the choices available, the more creative we can be in exercising those choices.

Insight - understanding of grammatical structure increases insight into the task, as when a writing task is clearly explained using appropriate grammatical terminology where this is relevant (e.g. "Write in the past tense and the first person.). One of the desirable characteristics of teaching in the KS3 Strategy is "direction: to ensure pupils know what they are doing, and why".

It is also possible that clearly defined writing tasks will be especially helpful for boys because "explicit grammatical knowledge ... provides an additional, more analytical dimension to the English curriculum which may appeal to those pupils, particularly boys, who are less interested in responses grounded in personal reaction" (from 'The Grammar Papers').

As well as helping improve students' writing skills, grammar teaching helps students to learn other languages more easily and helps students to improve their thinking skills. The Key Stage 3 English framework built on "the linguistic skills which pupils bring with them to the study of a modern language" and used the same glossary of grammatical terminology as MFL programmes of study.

The KS3 framework also recommended that students "develop critical thinking and problem solving through questioning, hypothesising, speculating and analysing"... the kinds of activities that take place when discussing or investigating grammar because students have to work out for themselves how the grammatical system works and how they can apply it to particular contexts.

There is, as we've already seen, a profound link between grammar and thinking, language and thought. The language we learn influences our cognitive development. Richard Hudson of UCL provides an example of this:

> A simple example is the grammatical choice between what and who (or between who and which); for example, English grammar compels us to decide whether or not an object in the distance is a person before we can put our question into words as: "What is that?" or "Who is that?" This repeated choice encourages us to divide the world into people and everything else (including other animals), in contrast with the scientific view that we take our place among the animals. Thinkers need to be aware of the pitfalls of relying on grammar.

Hudson goes on to say that grammar is a very special subject in the school curriculum because it has the potential for profound effects on a child's mental development. Children have a right to some understanding of how their language works, Hudson argues, which must inevitably include some grammar. Hudson supports his view in a number of ways:

> - Grammar is satisfying because it is such a highly-developed analytical system that (mostly) works well when applied to individual cases;
> - Grammar is interesting because it

allows us to explore a part of our minds whose structure is especially clear but also especially intricate and rich;
- Grammar gives status because having a grammar is often thought to be part of being a 'proper language'. In the KS3 Strategy, every kind of English has a grammar, so non-standard varieties may be discussed as well as standard English. The same argument could be applied to teaching about the grammar of community languages.

And that's why teaching SPaG in schools is important. But how best can it be taught..?

Chapter 5
How should we teach SPaG?

We've looked at what grammar is and why it should be taught in schools. Now let's consider how grammar should be taught.

In short, grammar teaching works best when it is:

✓ placed in context

✓ made relevant to students' writing

✓ made explicit as well as taught through investigations

✓ revisited systematically

✓ taught across the curriculum not confined to English lessons

Let's look at each of these factors in more detail...

Grammar should be taught as part of an integrated curriculum - not for its own sake. Grammar teaching should be **placed in context**, and grammatical features should be given purpose, effect, and meaning. As 'The Grammar Papers' says, grammatical knowledge should be "made relevant to the texts studied and written in class". Grammatical knowledge should be applied to a piece of writing, and ideally that writing should be a concrete and genuine example, not an example constructed by the teacher for the purposes of analysis.

Grammar teaching should be planned around grammatical concepts. As the National Literacy Strategy suggested, a lesson may be focused on a particular area of grammar, which allows systematic teaching; but the discussion of grammar then moves, via investigation, directly into writing, which makes it **relevant to students' writing**. Put simply, grammar teaching should be proactive, not reactive, but once a grammatical concept has been introduced, along with its terminology, the teacher is then free to use it reactively in commenting on students' writing.

Proactive teaching works well when looking at 'sentence combining', for example. The teacher writes a number of simple sentences on the board and students try to combine them into a single sentence in as many different ways as possible. The grammatical focus of this task is clear: the lesson teaches compound and complex sentences, and examines different types of clause. But this task also leads directly into a writing activity so grammar teaching is given purpose, effect, and meaning.

The KS3 Framework for English encourages students to explore grammar through **explicit teaching as well as through investigation**. It states that grammar teaching across the curriculum should be: direct and explicit; highly interactive; and inspiring and motivating. Grammar teaching in English, meanwhile, should be: more explicit, with attention being paid to 'word' and 'sentence' level skills; and should involve investigations in which pupils explore language and work out its rules and conventions.

Investigations are a great way to show students that grammar is real and not simply a list of terms. Indeed, it is important that our grammar teaching enables students to see the ideas behind the terms, and the connections between the ideas. Investigations encourage students to see the grammar behind everything they write. Take the humble noun, for instance. An investigation into the so-called *naming word* might conclude that: nouns are used to name people and objects; nouns may be common or proper; nouns may be singular or plural; nouns may also be used to name the actions that verbs can name; we can make nouns out of verbs; nouns may be modified by adjectives (but not by adverbs); nouns may be modified by determiners; nouns may be modified by prepositional phrases and relative clauses; and nouns may be used as the subjects and the objects of verbs. In short, to understand grammar is to understand sets of interconnecting facts.

All the grammatical knowledge that students have acquired should then be revisited as often as possible. 'The Grammar Papers' advises that "Teachers should base their planning on a clear idea of pupils' prior grammatical knowledge, to ensure that pupils are not taught the same aspects of grammar repeatedly and to make full use of pupils' implicit knowledge of grammar." **Revisiting and revising prior learning** helps students to consolidate their learning and helps create a permanent bank of well-understood ideas.

Grammar teaching is done best when it is not confined to English or MFL lessons but is **taught across the curriculum**. The National Literacy Strategy makes it clear that <u>the remit for grammar teaching lies with every teacher</u> in a school not just English and MFL teachers. 'The Grammar Papers' adds:

> "It is clear ... that explicit grammatical knowledge ... is relevant to other subjects in the way that knowledge is constructed. Although each subject has its own vocabulary and technical concepts, explicit grammatical knowledge can help students use the language of the subject area appropriately, for example when describing events, reporting a process, or explaining what they have learned."

The National Literacy Strategy produced a series of resources to help teachers deliver literacy across the curriculum. For example, the National Literacy Strategy documentation suggests a geography teacher might:

> - focus students' attention on the grammatical structures in an essay about the causes of famine by comparing different ways of using the word drought as a cause.
>
> - develop sensitivity to grammatical structure by exploring grammatical ways of connecting sentences that describe two kinds of valley.
>
> - prepare students for describing a geographical feature by pointing out that "many sentences will begin with adverbials to locate the feature, e.g. At the top ... , On one side ... , Above the snow-line ..."

And that is how we should teach grammar. But before we talk about the importance of SPaG in the current educational climate, let's first consider a few practical suggestions on how to teach spelling, punctuation, and grammar...

Teaching Spelling

If you want students to spell correctly you must first show them why accurate spelling is important. And why is spelling important? First and foremost, I would say, accurate spelling helps us to communicate more effectively with each other: correct spelling aids effective communication in that it ensures the reader understands what we're trying to say and helps to eliminate any confusion or misunderstanding. In an exam, for example, a student may have the right answer but their inaccurate spelling may confuse the examiner who is then unable to award the marks the response really deserves.

For students, spelling is also important because it is formally assessed and they will gain crucial marks for their spelling which could lead to a better class of qualification and, in turn, could provide a gateway to future success in life.

If spelling is important, why do some students find it so difficult?

There are many reasons why some students cannot spell. Some students have difficulty with spelling because they have a special learning need such as dyslexia. Others make mistakes because they spell phonetically, that is to say they spell words like they sound. For some words phonetic spelling is not a problem but for many others it is because the English language is not a phonetic one (many of our words derive from other languages and so are not spelt the way they sound). Other students have difficulty with spelling because they lack adequate reading experience: in effect, they have not had enough exposure to the written word. Some students have difficulty because they don't know how to learn spellings and don't have access to a range of spelling strategies because they're never been taught them. And, let's be honest, some students mis-spell words simply because they can't be bothered to check their work for accuracy before handing it in.

So how can we help students overcome their spelling difficulties? Traditionally, spelling has been taught by rote such as via the weekly spelling test whereby students are given a set of words to learn and are then assessed on those words in an oral test. Spelling tests still have an important part to play in helping students improve their spelling, particularly the spelling of key words, but the benefits of spelling tests tend to be short-lived and the words being assessed are taken often out of context. Instead, we need to combine our use of the spelling test (which you can still do, perhaps as a starter activity once a week) with a number of other strategies, including:

- Using **visual aids**: for example, the word 'bed' looks just like a bed when written down so why not draw a bed using the letters and display it on the wall? Memorising the visual appearance of words can really help some students so having key words on display, as well as labelling things in your classroom, is a good idea.

- Using **aural aids**: encourage students to *hear* the

similarities between words and to hear the common threads in 'families' of words such as 'advance', 'chance', and 'dance'.

- Study **etymology**: discuss how words are created, analyse Greek and Latin prefixes and suffixes, and so on.

- Use **dictionaries**: encourage students to look words up in a dictionary and model this process for them as often as possible.

- Encourage **reading**: do whatever you can to get students reading as frequently as possible and reading as many different text types as possible. Model this process by reading in public whenever you can.

- Share **strategies** for learning words by rote such as 'look-say-cover-write-check'.

- And finally, **cheat**: let students use the spellcheck function on word processing software whenever they write on a computer, laptop or tablet. Spellcheckers have their limits (they're not always to be trusted and cannot be relied upon in exams or when writing by hand) but they can be a means of helping students acknowledge their common spelling mistakes and can help students to learn the corrected spellings. Make sure the spellcheck function is set up so that mis-spelt words are underlined (and students have to right-click on the mis-spelt words in order to see the correct spelling or a set of suggestions) rather than being automatically corrected without the students' knowledge or active participation in the process.

And here are some strategies you can use to help students learn how to spell...

- **Words within words**: get students to look inside words to find as many other words as they can, like 'strum' in instrument.

- **Cut words up**: get students to split words into syllables so they can hear the hidden or silent letters, as in February which can be split as follows: Feb / ru / a / ry.

- **Teach word roots**: get students to recognise where words come from by studying etymology. For example, the word 'beautiful' is not spelt phonetically (if it was, it would be spelt something like this: 'buwteful') so it is helpful for students to know that the word derives from the French word 'beau' meaning handsome, which in turn comes from the Latin root 'bellus, which in English became 'beauty' and is then inflected by adding the suffix '-ful'. A study of common Latin and Greek root words is always useful and often very interesting. A starting point for this is to look at the numbers 1 to 10. In Latin, the numbers are: one = unus; two = duo; three = tres; four = quattuor; five = quinque; six = sex; seven = septem; eight = octo; nine = novem; and ten = decem. Once they know this, students can start to understand the names of some of our months and also the names given to some shapes.

- **Learn letter strings**: get students to recognise groups of letters that are commonly strung together like 'qu' and 'ch' and 'st', and 'ous' and 'ion' and 'ious' and so on.

- **Use mnemonics**: encourage students to learn mnemonics such as '**r**hythm **h**as **y**our **t**wo **h**ands **m**oving = rhythm' and '**b**ig **e**lephants **c**an **a**lways **u**pset **s**maller **e**lephants = because' in order to remember difficult spellings.

- **Pronounce words as they're spelt**: say all the letters in a word (including silent letters) such as -We-d-n-es-day' and 'li-s-t-en'.

Teaching Punctuation

The best way to teach punctuation is - as with spelling - to make students see just how important punctuation is as an aid to effective communication. Students need to know the reasons we use punctuation and these include the following:

- punctuation helps the reader by providing opportunities to pause, breathe and reflect;

- punctuation aids communication because it allows the reader to understand what someone is trying to say and in what tone or voice they are saying it.

Next, it's useful to understand why some students find punctuation so difficult to master. Reasons might include the following:

- Lack of experience: if a student has engaged in very little reading, they might not have had enough exposure to punctuation in order to use it themselves.

- Lack of understanding: if a student has never been taught the rules of punctuation, they may not understand how and when to use punctuation, nor even be able to recognise punctuation marks when they see them.

- Eagerness: if a student is enthusiastic about a piece of writing, they may get carried away and write pages and pages without paying much attention to the punctuation.

And then we need to help students learn the rules of punctuation. For example, we can:

- **Read work out loud**: this will help students to identify where punctuation needs to be added, either to improve the clarity of what is being said, or to help the reader to pace themselves.

- **Set achievable targets**: don't burden students with too many areas for improvement at any one time; instead, focus on smaller, more achievable steps such as 'use full stops at the end of every sentence' or 'use speech marks at the beginnings and ends of dialogue'.

- **Revisit the rules of punctuation as often as possible**: remind students of any pertinent rules of punctuation that they'll need to apply to the piece of writing they're working on or are about to start.

- **Encourage planning**: encourage students to plan their sentences in their heads before committing them to writing, thinking about where the punctuation needs to go.

Teaching Grammar

As with spelling and punctuation, grammar teaching works best when it is active and involves students, rather than being the product of didactic 'chalk and talk' teacher instruction. Perhaps, for example, students could work in groups or as a whole class, taking the role of the various parts of speech or of various types of clause in a sentence. They can physically move around in order to change the emphasis of a sentence or to create different types of sentence. Activities which engage students in the process of learning and involve physical movement like this, tend to have a greater chance of 'sticking' in students' heads. Here are some other ideas to consider:

- Identifying parts of speech: ask students to read through a text identifying all the adjectives (and then ask them analyse each adjective, stating how they think the word adds to the mood and atmosphere of the text). Alternatively, ask students to find synonyms (words which have a similar meaning) or antonyms (words which have an opposite meaning) for each adjective they find, discussing the effect on the text of making such changes.

- Exploring sentences and their effects: discuss how different types of sentence can have different effects on the tone and atmosphere of a piece of writing. For example, lots of consecutive simple sentences tend to create tension because they are short and sound breathless; whereas lots of complex sentences placed together (especially periodic sentences where the subject is placed at the end) create suspense because they make the reader wait before getting to the topic of the sentence.

- Run grammar competitions: engage students in competitions to find as many words as they can which start with certain prefixes or end with certain suffixes.

- Change tense and viewpoint: once students have completed a piece of writing, ask them to change the tense (from past to present continuous, for example) and the narrative viewpoint (from first to third person, for example) in order to see what effect is created.

- Write in stages: improve students' use of paragraphing by asking them to write a text one paragraph at a time and then set a limit on the number of sentences each paragraph can contain. Vary this limit so students can see the effect of using a variety of paragraph types.

- Synopses: ask students to summarise the key point made in each paragraph in a text in order to increase their awareness of how paragraphs fit together to make cohesive texts. This also helps students to see why writers start a new paragraph when they do (e.g. to signal a change of topic, a change of time, or for literary effect).

Helping students to make progress with SPaG

A good way to help students to improve the quality of their work is to include a SPaG-based objective for each extended piece of writing they do in class and for that objective to be levelled using level or grade/band descriptors. Here's a health warning first, though: I do not believe that objectives should be used as a means of placing a glass ceiling in the way of students (e.g. some students are told to aim for a level 4b whilst others are told to strive for a 5c in the manner of the 'all', 'most', 'some' style of objective). Rather, levelled objectives should be used in order to help *all* students make good progress by breaking down the key ingredients of SPaG. For example...

In terms of **spelling**, to achieve a Level 5, students need to: "spell *basic words* and *regular polysyllabic words* correctly". In other words, students should be able to spell words that follow spelling rules and fit into patterns with other words. Whereas, to get a Level 6, students need to: "spell *irregular polysyllabic words* correctly".

In terms of **punctuation**, to achieve a Level 5, students need to: "use *full stops, capital letters* and *question marks* accurately, use commas within a sentence, and use apostrophes and speech marks correctly". Whereas, for a Level 6, students need to: "use punctuation to develop *a range of complex sentences*".

In terms of **grammar**, to achieve a Level 5, students need to: "clearly structure [their] writing using *paragraphs*, use a range of *simple and complex sentences*, and use a wide range of vocabulary". Whereas, to get a Level 6, students need to: "show increasing control of *a range of sentence types*, and use *punctuation* *to clarify meaning and create effects*".

Sharing level descriptors in this way has the advantage of making SPaG explicit. It's a means of pulling back the curtain to reveal the man behind the wizard.

At its simplest, students can be taught that full stops, commas, and question marks are simple punctuation marks which need to be used correctly to achieve a Level 4 and higher, whereas colons and semi-colons are complex punctuation marks and if used correctly will allow students to access the higher levels (say, 6 and above) or grades. Breaking SPaG down in this way is a particularly useful tactic for boys and for those students who favour scientific approaches to English.

Chapter 6
Why is SPaG so important today?

Let's take stock: we've explored the history of grammar teaching and considered what SPaG is, why it should be taught and how it should be taught. Now let's put this into context. Why is SPaG particularly important at the moment?

SPaG's star is rising thanks to two significant changes:

1. School inspections

Firstly, there's a renewed focus on literacy in the 2012 Ofsted framework. Whatever your thoughts about Ofsted in general and their new inspection framework in particular, according literacy greater importance has got to be a good thing because without basic literacy skills students cannot be expected to access the curriculum in any subject.

The new inspection framework explains that, in order to make a judgment on the quality of the teaching of literacy, inspectors should evaluate "how well teaching enables pupils to develop skills in reading, writing, [and verbal] communication". Ofsted describes inadequate teaching in this area as being when "pupils cannot communicate, read, [and] write as well as they should". Exceptional performance in this area, by contrast, is described as being when pupils are able to "write in detail, develop ideas and look carefully at language, structure and presentation... make comparisons between texts including audience, purpose and form... [and] see when information is presented as argument or opinion".

Before we go any further, let's be clear about one thing: literacy as it appears in the Ofsted framework is not the same thing as English. Ofsted are clear that developing students' literacy skills is the responsibility of *all* teachers, irrespective of their subject specialism. Why? Because in order to access the curriculum in, say, science, students need to be able to read textbooks and research papers, and then write about their newly-acquired scientific knowledge in order to assimilate their learning and in order to demonstrate that learning. Likewise, students need to be able to communicate orally in order to contribute to classroom discussions in every subject area and, again, to demonstrate their learning across the curriculum.

2. Exam specifications

Secondly, SPaG is starting to find its way into national tests. At primary school, SPaG is now tested at the end of Key Stage 2 in place of the English SATs. At secondary school, SPaG is now part of the assessment criteria in GCSE English literature, history, geography and religious studies.

Primary SPaG[14]

In Year 6, new English spelling, punctuation, and grammar tests were introduced in May 2013 (in place of the English writing test previously taken at the end of Key Stage 2). The new SPaG tests cover those aspects of *spelling, punctuation, and grammar*, as well as *vocabulary*, which lend themselves to externally-marked testing, whilst *writing composition* is tested via teacher assessment. The SPaG tests are statutory in maintained schools, academies and free schools; therefore, primary schools must administer the tests for all children who have completed Key Stage 2 (usually at the end of Year 6) and are working at a Level 3 or above.

The Key Stage 2 tests assess elements of the current

---

[14] For a detailed exploration of the Key Stage 2 SPaG tests, see Appendix I.

English curriculum including:

✓ sentence grammar (through identification and grammatical accuracy);

✓ punctuation (through identification and grammatical accuracy);

✓ vocabulary (through grammatical accuracy); and

✓ spelling.

There are two tests: one for children working at Levels 3 to 5; and one for children working at Level 6. The Level 6 test has been designed to assess whether a child is working at a level 6 standard on the areas of the curriculum associated with spelling, punctuation, and grammar. This requires the assessment of elements of the Key Stage 3 programmes of study. Children being entered for the Level 6 test must already be working above a Level 5 and must have been following elements of the Key Stage 3 curriculum. Children sitting the Level 6 test must also be entered for the Level 3-5 test and if they do not pass the Level 6 test they will be awarded the result they achieved in the Level 3-5 test. Questions in the Level 6 test are more difficult and, to quote the DfE, are "designed to elicit responses that demonstrate a higher level of understanding on the part of the child than for the 3-5 test". The Level 6 test will include an extended response task, and a variety of question types which enable children to demonstrate their attainment more appropriately.

The primary school SPaG tests are to be completed on paper except for the spelling component which is carried out aurally. In the Level 3-5 test there are two components and in the Level 6 test there are three components. Not all components are strictly timed but the Standards and Testing Agency (STA) provide the following indications: the total testing time for each of the Level 3-5 and Level 6 tests should be around an hour. In the Level 3-5 test, the grammar, punctuation, and vocabulary test should last approximately 45 minutes and the spelling test should last about 15 minutes. In the Level 6 test, the extended task should last about 30 minutes, the grammar, punctuation, and vocabulary test around 20 minutes and the spelling test around 10 minutes.

Secondary SPaG

At secondary school, SPaG has been introduced into the assessment criteria of GCSE exams in subjects other than English.

SPaG has been added to the assessment criteria of four GCSE qualifications: English literature, history, geography, and religious studies[15]. These subjects were

---

[15] Please note that SPaG does not replace the Quality of Written Communication (QWC) mark, which remains in place in

chosen because they involve the reading and writing of extended prose texts. In each of these four qualifications, 5% of the total marks available in each exam are allocated to the assessment of students' ability to spell, punctuate, and use grammar correctly.

All the major exam boards use the same assessment criteria as prescribed by the Department for Education. But the marks they award each level of performance are different. AQA assesses SPaG out of 3 marks, where 3 marks is considered 'High Performance', 2 marks is considered 'Intermediate Performance' and 1 mark is considered 'Threshold Performance'. Edexcel assesses SPaG out of 4 marks where 4 marks is considered 'High Performance', 2 to 3 marks is considered 'Intermediate Performance' and 1 mark is considered 'Threshold Performance'. OCR assesses SPaG out of 9 marks where 7 to 9 marks is considered 'High Performance', 4 to 6 marks is considered 'Intermediate Performance' and 1 to 3 marks is considered 'Threshold Performance'.

The performance descriptors are as follows:

No marks awarded
Errors severely hinder the meaning of the response or candidates do not spell, punctuate or use the rules of grammar within the context of the demands of the question.

Threshold Performance

addition to the new SPaG assessment.

Candidates spell, punctuate and use the rules of grammar with reasonable accuracy in the context of the demands of the question. Any errors do not hinder meaning in the response. Where required, they use a limited range of specialist terms appropriately.

Intermediate Performance
Candidates spell, punctuate and use the rules of grammar with considerable accuracy and general control of meaning in the context of the demands of the question. Where required, they use a good range of specialist terms with facility.

High Performance
Candidates spell, punctuate and use the rules of grammar with consistent accuracy and effective control of meaning in the context of the demands of the question. Where required, they use a wide range of specialist terms adeptly and with precision.

If we decipher the assessment criteria, we might conclude that, at GCSE, SPaG is about:

✓ accurate spelling;

✓ effective use of punctuation to ensure clarity and to aid meaning;

✓ consistently obeying the rules of grammar; and

✓ effective use of a wide range of specialist (by which is meant 'subject specific') vocabulary.

This has significant implications for Humanities teachers (and for all teachers in the fullness of time).

English and Humanities teachers need to consider how they teach and assess students' spelling, especially the spelling of subject key words. They also need to consider how they reinforce and assess students' use of grammar such as using 'would have' not 'would of', as well as encouraging students to use formal written English with increasing confidence.

Edexcel suggests using literacy-based starters and plenaries (such as word games based on subject key words) as part of the drive to improve students' literacy skills. In terms of using specialist vocabulary, students need to be encouraged to write a glossary and to learn the definitions of key terms.

At GCSE, teachers need to balance the demands of teaching SPaG with the demands of teaching their specialist subject knowledge and skills. They also need to strike the right balance in the minds of their students.

Some students' literacy skills may be limited (or affected by their special educational needs) and yet their subject understanding may be impressive. It is possible for some students to be awarded full marks for their subject-specific responses but zero marks for SPaG. Teachers need to help students improve the quality of their spelling, punctuation, and grammar but must be careful that this doesn't hamper students' subject-based learning and that this doesn't demotivate students who enjoy the subject but find spelling, punctuation, and grammar challenging.

Chapter 7
SPaG? But I'm not an English teacher

In discussing why SPaG is important and how we should teach it, we will inevitably encounter the claim that SPaG is the responsibility of English teachers. Many of you will be thinking, 'If the English department got its act together, I wouldn't have to waste my time teaching kids to bloody punctuate, would I? I mean, I'm a bloody PE teacher, for god's sake. I should be shouting at the fat kid with the inhaler not talking about bloody semi-colons'. Or something like that.

Many teachers assume that SPaG is something members of the English department should teach. And, to some extent, they're right. But it is not only the domain of English teachers to ensure students learn and apply spelling, punctuation, and grammar rules, nor is it solely the English teacher's job to assess spelling, punctuation, and grammar whilst flagrant mistakes are ignored in every other subject.

But let's look at what English teachers in both primary and secondary schools <u>do</u> teach[16]...

SPaG is integral to the **primary** curriculum...

In the Early Years Foundation Stage, teachers are expected to: develop children's understanding and use of spoken language; introduce children to quality texts being read aloud; and encourage children to speak in sentences.

In Key Stage 1, teachers are expected to: introduce terminology where appropriate; extend children's experience of a wide range of quality texts, fostering an interest in words and word choices: engage children in word-play and in the investigation of language effects; and encourage children to write simple sentences using basic grammar.

In Key Stage 2, teachers are expected to: extend the range of appropriate terminology that children use, including all eight key word types (nouns, verbs, adjectives, adverbs,

[16] A caveat: the information here has been gleaned from the programmes of study in place at the time of writing (2013). There is currently a draft new National Curriculum for English being debated and finalised. This new curriculum is due to be taught from September 2014 onwards.

determiners, prepositions, pronouns and connectives); discuss authors' choices of words for effect, purpose, and meaning; extend children's uses of word-play within phrases, clauses, sentences and texts; and use more complex sentences, demonstrating an awareness of the effect on the reader of using particular word choices.

In EYFS, teachers are expected to teach SPaG throughout the day, every day in conversations, in dialogue during play, in modelling good use of spoken language, during story time, and in displays.

In Key Stage 1, teachers are expected to teach SPaG by modelling effective, quality spoken language, through shared texts, in reading aloud and guided reading, in literacy work such as word and sentence starters, through the use of 'word of the day' and in literacy in topic work.

In Key Stage 2, teachers are expected to teach SPaG by modelling, discussion, shared texts, reading aloud, guided reading, literacy teaching, through the use of shared success criteria, and the use of 'word of the day'.

In each case, it's important that SPaG is taught in context. In other words, children need to understand the context and purpose of grammar of grammar and punctuation and grammar teaching has to be part of the reading and writing curriculum so that children's understanding of grammatical terminology is seen as a means to an end, facilitating informed discussion about texts and effective writing of a range of texts.

Of course, there are further considerations to make. For EAL children, for example, SPaG teaching is more of a challenge: some of the eight word types may not exist in their first language and the word order they are familiar with may be at odds to English grammar. For hearing impaired children with a language delay, some of the eight word types may not yet be used in their spoken language or may sometimes be in a different order, in an incorrect tense or person. The best way to overcome such challenges is to establish children's speaking and listening skills first before focusing on reading and writing.

SPaG is also integral to the National Curriculum at **secondary** school...

In Key Stage 3, in terms of **sentences**, teachers are expected to teach: word order in complex sentences with one subordinate clause; defining relatives; reported speech; wh- questions. In Key Stage 4, in terms of sentences, teachers are expected to teach: word order with multiple subordinate clauses; conjunctions for contrast, reason, etc; conditional forms; non-defining relatives; participial clauses; more reported speech; embedded questions and tag questions. In Key Stage 5, for those students studying English language at A Level, teachers are expected to teach the following aspects of sentences: word order with wide range of subordinate clauses; conditional forms using had and would/could (etc.) have; comparative clauses; complex participial clauses; fronting and cleft sentences; more advanced reported speech, question tags, etc.

In terms of **noun phrases**, in Key Stage 3, students are expected to know about: pre and post modification; a range of determiners. In Key Stage 4, they are expected to know about: more complex pre and post modification; word order of determiners; definite, indefinite and zero articles; possessives. And in Key Stage 5, students are expected to know about: noun phrases of increasing complexity; zero article with countable and uncountable nouns.

In terms of **verb forms**, time markers, interrogatives, negatives and short forms, in Key Stage 3 , students are expected to know about: past, present, perfect; modals; phrasal verbs. In Key Stage 4, students are expected to know about: present perfect continuous; past perfect, simple passive; conditional would; causitive have and get; more modals, phrasal verbs. And in Key Stage 5, students are expected to know about: wide range of simple, continuous, perfect, perf. continuous verb forms; would expressing habit; modals for past obligation, etc.; wide range of phrasal verbs.

In terms of **adjectives**, in Key Stage 3, students are expected to know about: comparative and superlative;

compounds. In Key Stage 4, students are expected to know about: comparison; collocations of adjective plus preposition. In Key Stage 5, students are expected to know about: connotations and emotive strength of adjectives; wider range of collocations.

In terms of **adverbs and prepositional phrases**, in Key Stage 3, students are expected to know about: range of prepositional phrases; expressions of certainty; intensifiers. In Key Stage 4, students are expected to know about: concession; collocates of verbs and prepositions; collocates of nouns and prepositions; adverbial phrases; comparative, superlative adverbs. In Key Stage 5, students are expected to know about: more intensifiers; prepositions and -ing form; prepositions followed by noun phrases.

And, finally, in terms of **discourse markers**, Key Stage 3 students are expected to know about: addition, sequence, contrast; vagueness. Key Stage 4 students are expected to know about: cause and effect; spoken discourse markers. Key Stage 5 students are expected to know about: logical markers; sequence markers.

At Key Stage 3, the English programmes of study are divided into three areas: reading, writing, and speaking and listening. Each area is again subdivided. For example, writing is subdivided into 'composition' and 'technical accuracy'. We will focus our attentions on these two areas as they relate directly to SPaG.

Let's begin with **Writing Composition**

In English at Key Stage Three, students follow programmes of study which are designed to help them to:

- write clearly and coherently, including an appropriate level of detail

- write imaginatively, creatively and thoughtfully, producing texts that interest and engage the reader

- generate and harness new ideas and develop them in their writing

- adapt style and language appropriately for a range of forms, purposes and readers

- maintain consistent points of view in fiction and non-fiction writing

- use imaginative vocabulary and varied linguistic and literary techniques to achieve particular effects

- structure their writing to support the purpose of the task and guide the reader

- use clearly demarcated paragraphs to organise meaning

- use complex sentences to extend, link and develop ideas

- vary sentence structure for interest, effect and subtleties of meaning

- consider what the reader needs to know and include

relevant details

- use formal and impersonal language and concise expression

- develop logical arguments and cite evidence

- use persuasive techniques and rhetorical devices

- form their own view, taking into account a range of evidence and opinions

- present material clearly, using appropriate layout, illustrations and organisation

- use planning, drafting, editing, proofreading and self-evaluation to shape and craft their writing for maximum effect

- summarise and take notes

- write legibly, with fluency and, when required, speed.

Now let's look at **Writing Technical Accuracy**

In English at Key Stage Three, students follow programmes of study which are designed to help them to:

- use the conventions of standard English effectively

- use grammar accurately in a variety of sentence types, including subject–verb agreement and correct and consistent use of tense

- signal sentence structure by the effective use of the full range of punctuation marks to clarify meaning

- spell correctly, increasing their knowledge of regular patterns of spelling, word families, roots of words and derivations, including prefixes, suffixes and inflections.

It is reasonable, therefore, for teachers of subjects other than English to assume that the above will be taught in English. Teachers of other subjects need to reinforce this learning and certainly need to ensure they do not contradict it.

Let's look at what else teachers of subjects other than English need to do...

Literacy across the curriculum

In addition to the SPaG that's taught in English, all subject teachers are responsible for improving levels of literacy and for explicitly teaching and assessing students' literacy skills. So what is literacy? There are some common misunderstandings around this term. Many use the words 'literacy' and 'English' synonymously but they are different. Ofsted define 'literacy' as a "combination of skills in reading, writing and oracy [or verbal communication]". The National Literacy Trust provides the following advocacy statement:

> "Literacy skills are essential for young people to reach their potential in school and [for] fulfilling opportunities throughout life. Every school needs a rigorous whole-school literacy policy which is implemented systematically across the curriculum and all teachers should view themselves as teachers of literacy, regardless of their subject specialism. Some schools have achieved this and as a result young people are able to not only access the curriculum, but have the tools to extend their thinking and knowledge with outstanding results."

The crucial phrase here is that "all teachers should view themselves as teachers of literacy, regardless of their subject specialism". Teaching literacy is not the same as teaching English. Literacy is about helping students to access the whole curriculum. Literacy is about helping students to read subject information and helping students to write in order that they can assimilate that information and then demonstrate their learning.

Teaching literacy might take the form of:

✓ displaying key words;

✓ writing three key words for each lesson on the white board at the start of the lesson and reinforcing the meaning and usage of these words throughout the lesson;

- ✓ giving students the opportunity to say key words out loud, then asking them to write a sentence using the word in context;

- ✓ giving students the opportunity to repeat a new skill;

- ✓ providing students with workbooks to record new vocabulary – like a personal subject dictionary;

- ✓ providing cut-up sentences on a subject-specific topic and asking students to reconstruct them;

- ✓ analysing the audience, purpose and style of the texts being studied;

- ✓ providing opportunities for group discussion and debate, reinforcing the rules of effective group talk.

Teaching literacy, you will see, is not a case of doing an English teacher's job for them... it means helping students to access and understand your subject and helping students to engage in classroom discussions and debate.

*

So much for the theory... let's put SPaG into practice.

We now know a little of the history of SPaG teaching in England; we know what SPaG is, why we should teach it, and how we should teach it; and we know the ways in which SPaG is now being assessed in both primary and secondary schools. But there is an elephant in the room...

How confident are you about your own grasp of the rules of spelling, punctuation, and grammar?

After all, it's helpful to know what SPaG is and what aspects of it we need to teach... but all this theory is rendered meaningless if your own grasp of the rules of spelling, punctuation, and grammar is, well, not as firm as it should be.

If you do not know a dangling participle when it's dangling in front of your very eyes, how can you be expected to spot one in your students' work?

If you don't recognise a subordinate clause when it

walks right up to you in the street wearing a 'Frankie Says Subordinate Clause' tee-shirt and shouting "I'm a subordinate clause, you fool" in your face, then what hope have you of teaching your students how to write in a range of complex sentences?

And yet... and yet...

Admitting you don't know your adverbs from your elbow is not easy. Lots of teachers lack a basic understanding of grammar (let's not forget that most of today's teachers were not themselves taught grammar at school) and yet are too embarrassed to ask for help. That is where Part Two of this book comes in... so let's take a look at SPaG in practice. Let's answer all those embarrassing questions about spelling, punctuation, and grammar you've always been afraid to ask for fear of being banished to the corner of the staffroom with a coned hat on your head and a 'kick me' post-it stuck to your back...

PART TWO

SPaG in practice

"The English language is a common thief, slyly pickpocketing linguistic features from every foreign tourist it passes in the street."

Chapter 8
Teaching SPaG isn't easy

Before we dig out the daunting dentist's drill and set screechingly to work filling all those niggling little gaps in your grammatical knowledge, let's first recline your chair, apply the gas mask gently to your mouth and massage your ego a little... after all, you're not alone in saying 'you and I' when you really mean 'you and me'... And, what's more, it's not your fault! Your spelling slips, punctuation faux pas, and grammatical gaffes are probably the result of two factors, both of which are outside your control:

1 You weren't taught grammar when you were at school; and

2 English grammar is bloody stupid!

Let's explore each of those factors...

Lack of grammar instruction

I believe the gap in teachers' knowledge is, in part, due to the fact that grammar was not explicitly taught in schools in the 1960s, '70s and '80s, a time when many of today's teachers were educated. Most teachers can read and write well but cannot access the metalanguage they need in order to identify and define linguistic concepts like subordinate clauses and past participles. If this describes you, never fear: not only are you in good company, but by the end of this book you'll be a grammar expert, marching down the high street, red pen in hand, ready to correct ~~grocer's~~ ~~grocers's~~ grocers' apostrophes with assuredness and panache!

You call that a language?

Of course, there is another reason why some teachers' knowledge of the rules of spelling, punctuation, and grammar has more holes in it than a piece of Swiss cheese stuck to a dartboard! And that is because English is an odd language, at times seemingly nonsensical. If you don't believe me, try reading the following sentences aloud without first practising them:

> *We must polish the Polish furniture.*
> *He could lead if he would get the lead out.*
> *The farm was used to produce produce.*

The dump was so full that it had to refuse more refuse.

After dessert, the soldier decided to desert his post in the desert.

No time like the present to present the present.

A bass and a trout were painted on the head of the bass drum.

When shot at, the dove dove into the bushes.

I did not object to the object.

The insurance was invalid for the invalid.

The bandage was wound around the wound.

There was a row among the oarsmen about how to row.

They were too close to the door to close it.

The buck does funny things when the does are present.

They sent a sewer down to stitch the tear in the sewer line.

To help with planting, the farmer taught his sow to sow.

The wind was too strong to wind the sail.

After a number of injections my jaw got number.

Upon seeing the tear in my clothes I shed a tear.

I had to subject the subject to a series of tests.

How can I intimate this to my most intimate friend?

I live next to the stadium where bands play live.

A minute is a minute part of a day.

Starting to understand how some of your students feel when reading aloud in class? And yet if you thought English just couldn't get any stranger than that, then consider this oddity of the English language...

The letters '-ough' can be pronounced in myriad different ways, as the following passage proves:

A rough-coated, dough-faced, thoughtful ploughman strode through the streets of Scarborough; after falling into a slough, he coughed and hiccoughed.

Why is this? Why is English such an odd language?

The English language is like a sponge in that it soaks up words from other languages. Put less diplomatically, it is a common thief, slyly pickpocketing linguistic features from every foreign tourist it passes in the street!

A basic understanding of the history of our language is helpful in understanding how it works. So, let's take a trip down memory lane and hold the world's hand as she gives birth to a language that - despite its inauspicious beginnings - will, in time, grow up to become the world's *lingua franca*[17]...

---

[17] ...although it would have to borrow the phrase 'lingua franca' from Latin in order to pithily describe itself as a language that is widely used as a means of communication by speakers of other languages because it doesn't have a pithy phrase of its own which means 'a language that is widely used as a means of communication by speakers of other languages' and it's not very pithy to say that 'English would grow up to become a language that is widely used as a means of communication by speakers of other languages'. If you see what I mean.

Chapter 9
The life and times of English

The English language is about 13 centuries old, which is slightly older than Cliff Richard. There are written records in English dating back to approximately 700AD but that language is unrecognisable from the one we use today. If you want to compare the two, read *Beowulf* which is the oldest surviving example of Old English (or Anglo-Saxon) there is. Here's a short sample:

Fæder ure þuþe eart on heofonum

si þin nama gehalgod tobecume þin rice

gewurþe

þin willa on eorðan swa swa on heofonum

urne gedæghwamlican hlaf syle us to dæg

and forgyf us ure gyltas swa swa we forgyfað urum gyltendum

and ne gelæd þu us on costnunge ac alys us of

yfele soþlice.

Need I say more?

English is a Germanic language belonging to the Indo-European family of languages. Today, it is the second most widely spoken language in the world with more than 400 million native speakers, plus another 350 million people who speak it as a second language and a further 100 million people who use it as a foreign language. My 'back of an envelope' calculation informs me that an estimated 1.9 billion people - which is an impressive one-third of the earth's population - possess some knowledge of the English language. Moreover, English is listed as the official language of over 45 countries and is spoken extensively in many more countries than that where it is a semi-official language. French is probably the next biggest language but is only spoken in 27 countries. Not that I'm competitive. Or hate the French.

Let's look at how this king of languages came to be so dominant...

Old English (or Anglo-Saxon)

Until the Fifth Century AD, the British Isles were

inhabited by the Celts. But in the Fifth Century they were invaded by three Germanic peoples called the Angles, the Saxons, and the Jutes. These peoples came from what is now Denmark and northern Germany. The language spoken by the Jutes (from Jutland) and the Angles (from Engle) was called *Enlisc* from which our word 'English' derives.

The Celtic inhabitants were forced to the northern and western extremities of Britain by the invaders and settled in what is now Cornwall, Wales, and Scotland. The Celts continued to speak Celtic from which the Cornish, Welsh, and Scots Gaelic languages are derived. One group of Celts moved south to France where their Celtic language evolved into Breton (the language of Brittany).

The Saxons went on to form the South Saxon Kingdom (or Sussex), the West Saxon Kingdom (or Wessex) and the East Saxon Kingdom (Essex). The Jutes and the Angles, meanwhile, settled in the central part of southern England and along the northern and eastern coasts thus forming the kingdoms of Kent, East Anglia, Mercia, and Northumbria, which together formed Engle-land (or Angle land) from which we derive the word *England*.

In the Ninth Century, a Viking invasion (or rather a series of Viking invasions) transformed the linguistic landscape as well as the political one: all the kingdoms bar Wessex were usurped. Because Wessex remained independent, the West Saxon dialect became the official language of

Britain.

Old English is so different to the language we speak today largely because Old English (or Anglo-Saxon as it is also known) used the Runic alphabet (borrowed from Scandinavia) not the Latin alphabet we use today. The Latin alphabet was brought over from Ireland by Christian missionaries and has remained the writing system of English ever since.

Old English words came from an Anglo-Saxon base with additional words borrowed from Latin and also from the Scandinavian languages, Danish and Norse. Although the Vikings added many Norse words to our language, a great number of Celtic words survived in the form of place names and the names of physical features of the landscape. Today, the English language we speak is approximately half Germanic and Scandinavian, and half French and Latin.

Initially, many English and Norse words co-existed, giving rise to pairs of words which meant the same thing, such as 'nay' and 'no', 'ill' and 'sick', and 'anger' and 'wrath'.

Middle English

In 1066 - a date etched on every schoolchild's memory - the Normans invaded Britain from northern France and quickly and unceremoniously ended Anglo-Saxon's reign in England. William the Conqueror was crowned King William I and English fell under the influence of a new, largely French language. For example, many new words entered the language at this time from Norman French, Parisian French and Scandinavian. Between 1066 and 1400, Latin, French, and English were spoken alongside each other. Many French and English words co-existed, such as 'annual' and 'yearly', and 'close' and 'shut, and 'reply' and 'answer'.

English almost disappeared because French and Latin dominated our system of government as well as the legal system. But English bounced back and was declared the official language of these isles in 1362. Later in the Fourteenth Century, English became the dominant language of the British Isles once more. In 1399 King Henry VI became the first king since before the Norman Conquest for whom English was a first language. By the end of the Fourteenth Century, the regional dialect of English spoken in London and the South East became the standard dialect known as Middle English, the language of Geoffrey Chaucer. Chaucer's *Canterbury Tales* provides us with a flavour of Middle English. Here, for example, is an extract from the beginning of *The Wife of Bath*:

> *Here bigynneth the Tale of the Wyf of Bathe.*
> *In tholde dayes of the Kyng Arthour,*
> *Of which that Britons speken greet honour,*
> *All was this land fulfild of Fayerye.*

The elf-queene, with hir joly compaignye,
Daunced ful ofte in many a grene mede;
This was the olde opinion, as I rede.

It's much easier to follow than Beowulf but still some distance from the language we use today.

Early Modern English

The language began to be standardised throughout the Fifteenth, Sixteenth and Seventeenth Centuries. The London dialect became the language spoken by the upper classes and was the dialect chosen by William Caxton as the language of written English when he introduced the printing press to England in 1476. Thus, books were written in the London dialect, or London Standard, now known as *standard English*. Thanks to the printing press, English spelling and grammar became increasingly standardised, a process that hastened somewhat following the publication of the first English Dictionary by Samuel Johnson in 1604.

Early Modern English was highly influenced by Greek and Latin - in part, as a result of the growth of the British Empire and the Renaissance of classical learning. For example, we added many prefixes and suffixes to our language at this time and most of them derived from Greek and Latin.

The expansion of the Empire facilitated an equally vast expansion in our vocabulary because we had to find words to describe all the new things we were discovering and inventing. Shakespeare is a great example of this spirit of invention (and theft). He borrowed heavily words imported from France and Italy and, when he couldn't find a word which suited his purpose, he simply made one up. As a result, Shakespeare invented (or *coined*) around 2000 words, many of which we still use today. Although, sadly, the phrase 'twangling pigeon-livered flibblertigibbet' is no longer in common usage.

It wasn't just our vocabulary that was changing. The way we pronounced those words was also being transformed. Most notably, as a result of a process called The Great Vowel Shift. The way we pronounced the five vowels (a, e, i, o, u) shifted greatly (I suppose that's why they called it the Great Vowel Shift). In most cases - though not all - the pronunciation shifted from the way the French say their vowels (a) to the way we say them today (A).

Modern English

Our language evolved into Modern English - the language we speak today - in the Seventeenth Century although English - like all languages - is very different today than it was in, say, 1650. Indeed, it is evolving all the time. The main difference between Early Modern English and Modern English was the way we inflected verbs. For example, the verb form which ended in 'th' changed to 's', as in 'loveth' which became 'loves', and 'hath' which became 'has'.

The colonisation of America had a major influence on our language, too. Initially, British English and American English were very similar but (as a result of the same process that British English underwent following the Norman Conquest) differences started to proliferate as dialects were no longer repressed and standards were relaxed. Many spellings were simplified so that their spelling more closely matched the way words were pronounced, as in centre = center, cheque = check, gaol = jail, and tyre = tire.

Another major influence on the development of English in the modern age was the industrial revolution, followed by the scientific and technological revolutions. New words (or neologisms) had to be created to describe new inventions and concepts. This book, for example, may have reached you in the form of an *eBook* which you *downloaded* from the *Internet* on your *PC* or *iPad* for viewing on your *Kindle* or similar *e-reading* device. And once you've read this book, you might want to *email* me, or send me a *tweet* on *Twitter*, or like my page on *Facebook*. You get the picture... with each new idea comes a set of new words.

English continues to evolve as it becomes more dominant as a world language - particularly as the language of international business and diplomacy - and, as it spreads, so it becomes more varied and fragmented just like Latin became fragmented into French, Spanish and Italian over a thousand years ago.

Just why English has become so dominant and continues to do so is a bit of a mystery, though. It's even more mysterious when you consider what a complex and difficult language it is to learn. Its grammar is grossly complicated; its spelling silly; its pronunciation peculiar. In the pro's column, English is no longer accented like French and Spanish, its spelling system is closely connected to that of many European languages and so is easier for European speakers to pick up, it's grammar is flexible, too, allowing us to rearrange words to alter the emphasis, and it uses single consonants which usually represent the same sounds and so are easily understood. But in the con's column: its alphabet is limited and does not represent all the sounds we need, and its spelling system is not based on its system of pronunciation but on its foreign language origins and so it is impossible to learn the language phonetically.

We've taken a brief tour through the history of the English language and have a better understanding of why the language is so complicated and peculiar. So now let's take a look at some of those complications and peculiarities... let's improve our knowledge of the language's odd spelling, punctuation and grammar rules...

Chapter 10
The building blocks of English[18]

The key to understanding the English language is to treat it like building a house: before you can move your furniture in, you have to dig the foundations out then lay the bricks layer by layer, storey by storey.

Those layers are made up of the following components:

---

[18] WARNING: Laboured metaphor ahead!

Letters
fit together to make
Phonemes and morphemes
fit together to make
Words
fit together to make
Phrases
fit together to make
Clauses
fit together to make
Sentences
fit together to make
Paragraphs
fit together to make
Texts

Let's look at each component in turn...

Chapter 11
Words[19]

Words are not the smallest units of sound or meaning. Words are made up of letters and letters combine to form phonemes and morphemes (and graphemes[20], for that matter) which then combine to form words.

For example, pre- is a **morpheme** because it contains meaning even though it is not a word in its own right. It is a prefix which means 'previous to' or 'before'. So pre-1990 means before the year 1990.

-ch is a **phoneme** because it is a combination of letters which together make one sound (as in the -ch in church)

[19] Contrary to what Elton John said, 'sorry' is not the hardest word; it's *pneumonoultramicroscopicsilicovolcanoconiosis*. According to the Oxford English Dictionary, this 45-letter word is a supposed lung disease.

[20] A grapheme is a unit of writing language.

but, again, it is not a word.

But words are a good starting point for our understanding of SPaG and so this is where we shall begin...

There are four main word classes (which are sometimes called the parts of speech): nouns, verbs, adjectives, and adverbs. In addition, there are pronouns which are words we use in place of nouns. And then there are function words - words which help us to create sentences that make sense - such as connectives, prepositions and determiners. Let's start with the word classes...

NOUNS

A noun is a naming word which identifies a person, an object, an idea, concept or emotion.

There are several different types of noun (and a noun can belong to more than one category), as follows:

Common noun

A common noun is a name that refers to people, places or objects *in general* such as 'man', 'town' and 'table'.

Proper noun

A proper noun is a name that refers to people, places or objects *in particular* such as 'John', 'London' and 'January'.

Concrete noun

A concrete noun is a name which identifies tangible objects: in other words, things that exist physically and can be seen, heard, smelt, touched, or tasted, such as 'table', 'cat', and 'song'.

Abstract noun

An abstract noun is a name which identifies ideas, concepts and emotions: in other words, things that cannot be seen, heard, smelt, touched or tasted, but can be felt or thought, such as 'happiness', 'democracy' and 'truth'.

Collective nouns

Collective nouns refer to groups of people or things, such as 'family', 'government', and 'herd'. Contrary to popular belief, collective nouns can *usually* be treated as either singular or plural and therefore can be accompanied by either a singular or plural verb. For example, "The team was outplayed" and "The team were outplayed" are both grammatically correct. But, whichever form you choose, it's important to be consistent throughout the text. Pick your favourite and stick to it!

VERBS

A verb is a doing word in that it describes what a person or thing does or what happens. For example, verbs can describe an action, an occurrence, or a change. A verb's basic form is called the **infinitive** and is usually preceded by 'to', as in 'to walk' and 'to talk'. And this is where it starts to get a bit complicated...

The **tense** of a verb tells you *when* something was done. There are three main tenses:

- present (I am, he is, they are)

- past (I was, he was, they were)

- future (I will/shall, he will, they will)

The three main tenses can be subdivided, as follows:

- the present continuous – he is talking

- the past continuous – he was talking

- the future continuous – he will be talking

- the present perfect – he has talked

- the present perfect continuous – he has been talking

- the past perfect – he had talked

- the past perfect continuous – he had been talking

- the future perfect – he will have talked

- the future perfect continuous – he will have been talking

A verb's tense is changed (the term for this process is *inflection,* so we say that verbs are *inflected)* by adding either -ed or -ing to the basic form (or 'stem'), or by introducing other supporting verbs such as 'am', 'was', 'have', 'has', 'had', 'will' and 'shall'. These words are called **auxiliary verbs** because they support the main verb just like auxiliary nurses support the work of nurses.

Most verbs are inflected in the way described above and are therefore called **regular verbs**. So, for example, the verb *talk* is changed like this:

Verb = talk

Third person singular present tense = he talks

Third person singular past tense = he talked

Past participle = talked

Present participle = talking

But, this being English, there are some exceptions to the rule. Verbs which do not follow this pattern are called **irregular verbs**. Here are some examples...

Verb = go

Third person singular present tense = he goes

Third person singular past tense = he went

Past participle = gone

Present participle = going

Verb = begin

Third person singular present tense = he begins

Third person singular past tense = he began

Past participle = begun

Present participle = beginning

Verb = take

Third person singular present tense = he takes

Third person singular past tense = he took

Past participle = taken

Present participle = taking

Subject - verb - object

A subject is an active person or thing, the person or thing doing something or the person or thing the sentence is about. The subject usually comes before the verb, as in "The cat sat on the mat" where the 'cat' is the subject (the do-er) and 'sat' is the verb (the doing).

In interrogative sentences (that is to say, sentences that are questions), the subject usually comes after the verb as in "How old is the cat?" where the 'cat' is the subject and 'is' is the verb 'to be'.

In imperative sentences (that is to say, sentences that convey a demand or command), the subject is not usually stated explicitly but is understood implicitly or is inferred, as in: "Stop doing that!" where implicitly the subject is 'you' (You stop doing that).

An object is the passive person or thing, a person or thing that is done to, a person or thing that is affected by the subject's actions. For example, in "The cat sat on the mat", the 'mat' is the object because it is being sat upon by the cat.

There are direct objects and indirect objects. Direct objects are so-called because they are directly affected by the verb. The 'mat' in the previous paragraph is a direct object because it is directly affected by being sat upon; it is passive because it does not itself do anything and has no choice but to be sat upon (poor mat).

An indirect object is usually the person or thing that gains something from the action of the verb. For example, in the sentence "Janet fed the cat some fish", the cat is the indirect object because it has been given some fish. The fish is the direct object because it has been fed to the cat ('fed' being the verb).

Can there possibly be any other kinds of verb? I hear you cry. Well, yes, I fear there is...

There are transitive and intransitive verbs, for starters. **Transitive verbs** are those which are used with an object, as in "I love your hat" where 'love' is a transitive verb attached to the object 'hat'. Transitive verbs can be used with either a direct object or an indirect object or with both, as in "John sent her a card" where 'her' is the indirect object and 'card' is the direct object.

An **intransitive verb**, by contrast, is not followed by an object, as in "We talked all night" where 'talked' is an intransitive verb.

Some words can act as either intransitive or transitive verbs - such as 'to leave' which in the sentence "He left town" acts as an intransitive verb whereas in the sentence "He wanted to leave early" acts as a transitive verb.

A **participle** is a word created by inflecting a verb (by adding -d, -ed or -ing). There are two breeds of participle: the **present participle** which ends with -ing because it is *happening* now; the **past participle** which ends in -d or -ed for regular verbs (or with -t or -en for most irregular verbs) because it *happened* in the past. Participles can also be combined with auxiliary verbs to make the present continuous ("I am walking to town") and the past perfect ("I had walked to town"). Participles can also be used as adjectives as in "The floor was covered in _broken_ crockery" and as a noun as in "John was told to do more _walking_". When a present participle is used as a noun (like 'walking' was in the last sentence) it is called a **gerund** but let's not get carried away with ourselves. Gerunds are for another day so let's *gerund* with more important matters...

Verbs can also be in the **active voice** (whereby the subject of the verb is doing the action, as in "England *beat* Germany on penalties") or in the **passive voice** (whereby the subject experiences the action but does not do it, as in "Germany were *beaten* on penalties" - here the point of view has been changed and Germany is the subject of the passive verb 'beaten').

Sometimes verbs are made up of more than one word. These are called verbal phrases or phrasal verbs, whichever you prefer! Usually, a main verb is combined with an adverb or a preposition as in "John fell down the stairs" where 'fell' is the main verb and 'down' is a preposition and together they make a verbal phrase.

We've already met auxiliary verbs (such as 'be' and 'do') and know that they help to form different verb tenses as in "John *had spoken* to Janet". But there is another set of auxiliary verbs called **modal verbs** (such as should, shall, will; can, ought, could; will, would; must, may, might) which *modify* the main verb.

And that, you'll be relieved to hear, is all you need to know about verbs for now. Take a deep breath, dust yourself down and let's tackle adjectives...

ADJECTIVES

An adjective describes a noun. For example, "A black cat" and "An English rose". When adjectives are placed before the noun like this, they are called **attributive** adjectives. When they are placed after a verb (as in "The cat is black" and "The rose was English") they are called **predicative** adjectives.

Adjectives come in three different forms: the **absolute**; the **comparative**; and the **superlative** as in *big, bigger and biggest,* or *small, smaller and smallest.*

ADVERBS

The word 'adverb' is itself a big clue as to its function: it is a *blend* word, created by squeezing two words into one another. The two words are *adjective* and *verb* and, as such, adverbs describe an action. For example, "He talked quickly" where 'quickly' is the adverb because it describes how the talking was done. Adverbs can also be used to indicate where something occurs as in "I travel abroad" where 'abroad' is the adverb describing where the travel is done. Adverbs can also strengthen or weaken a verb or adjective as in "I really want to" where 'really' is an adverb strengthening the verb 'want to' and "I hardly noticed" where 'hardly' weakens the verb 'noticed'.

When an adverb refers to a whole statement rather than just a part of it, it is called a **sentence adverb**, as in "Unfortunately, I could not attend the ceremony" where 'unfortunately' is an adverb which refers to the statement that follows it.

And that's it for the word classes which are all very important but are useless without the help of function words, words which help string sentences together. I like to think of word classes as boxers and function words as the little men in woolly hats who sit on stools just outside the ring chewing gum and occasionally throwing buckets of water over the boxers before pushing them back into the ring to get beaten up.

PRONOUNS

Pronouns are words which are used in place of a noun (the noun has usually been mentioned before or is already known or inferred). Pronouns are used to help avoid repeating a noun which can sound ugly or boring (a bit like Piers Morgan). For example, "John took his laptop out with him" where 'him' is a pronoun being used in place of John. Without the pronoun the sentence would sound silly and ungainly: "John took his laptop out with John".

Personal pronouns are used in place of nouns which refer to specific people or objects. Here's a list of the most common personal pronouns: I, me, mine, you, yours, his, her, hers, we, us, our, they, and them. Those personal pronouns which act as the subject of verbs (I, you, we, he, she, it, we, and they) are, rather sensibly, called **subjective pronouns**. Those which act as the object of verbs (me, you, us, him, her, it, and them) are - no less sensibly - called **objective pronouns**. Note that some pronouns can act as either subject or object.

CONNECTIVES

Connectives (which are also called *conjunctions*) connect parts of a sentence to each other. There are two types of connective: a **coordinating connective** joins parts of a sentence that are equal in value to each other (e.g. "In PE we play football *and* rugby" and "You can read the book *or* listen to the audiobook"); and **subordinating connectives** which connect subordinate clauses to main clauses (e.g. "The cat sat on the mat *because* she was tired"). And, despite what you may have heard, it is perfectly acceptable to start a sentence with a connective like 'and'.

PREPOSITIONS

Prepositions show the relationship between words in a sentence, often to indicate where something is in relation to something else (e.g. "The cat was *under* the table" and "The letter arrived *on* Monday"). Here are some examples to help you: on, in, under, over, up, down, between, after, with, by, when.

DETERMINERS

Determiners are words which introduce a noun: the most common are 'the', 'a', 'an', 'this', 'these' and 'those'. 'The' is the king of the determiners, is very sure of itself, and is called the **definite article**. 'A' is the queen, a bit of a prevaricator, and is called the **indefinite article**.

Another class of determiner is the possessive determiner which, as the name suggests, indicates possession. Examples of possessive determiners include the words 'my', 'your', 'our', 'his', 'her', and 'their'.

And that's all you need to know about the word classes and function words. But before we begin joining words together like building blocks, let's stop to consider how words are made and changed. This is called...

Chapter 12
Etymology

We've already looked at how words are **inflected**. That is to say, how words are altered by changing their number from singular to plural, or by changing their tense from present to past or future. Now let's look at how words are altered by adding letters at their beginning and end so that their meaning is changed. This process is called affixation.

The root word to which we add extra bits is called the *stem*. A set of letters that is added to the beginning of a word is called a **prefix** and a set of letters that is added to the end of a word is called a **suffix**. For example, the stem word 'happy' can be changed by adding the prefix 'un' to the beginning of it to become 'unhappy'. Adding this prefix gives the word its opposite meaning. The prefix 'dis' is another common way of opposing a word's meaning, as in 'dissatisfied' which is the opposite of 'satisfied'. Prefixes usually change a word's meaning.

Suffixes usually change a word from one word class to another. For example, a word can change from being a verb to an adjective by adding the suffix '-able' or '-ible' as in "loveable" which changes from the verb 'to love' to the adjective describing someone as 'loveable'. The suffix '-ise' or 'ize' changes a word from a noun to a verb, as in "specialise". But more than this later...

So, that's how to expand words using prefixes and suffixes. But some words are not expanded ; they are shortened... words which are cut short are called **abbreviations** and there are several types of abbreviation it's good to know...

Shortenings are abbreviations in which the beginning and/or end of a word has been cut off. For example, 'flu' is a shortened form of 'influenza' and 'blog' is a shortened form of 'weblog'. Many shortenings - like these two examples - no longer require an apostrophe to show where letters have been cut off because the shortened word has taken on the status of a word in its own right, rather than an abbreviation. It's perfectly acceptable to use an apostrophe, for example with 'flu, but the apostrophe is superfluous. Other shortenings involve a different spelling as in 'bike' which is short for 'bicycle'.

Contractions are a type of abbreviation whereby letters are taken away from the middle of the word. For example, "Ltd" is a contraction of 'limited'. Other contractions, like 'don't', are abbreviated forms of more than one word - in this case, of the words 'do' and 'not'. In all cases where the contraction represents more than one word, an apostrophe should be used to indicate where the letters have been omitted <u>not</u> where the two words conjoin.

Initialisms are abbreviations which take the initials of words which are then pronounced as separate letters, like BBC and ITV. It is acceptable to use full stops between the initials (as in B.B.C.) although this is a matter of stylistics and can be omitted. Today, it is more common to leave the full stops out. When pluralising an initialism, you should not use an apostrophe - so it should be "a group of MPs" not "a group of MP's". An apostrophe should only be used to show possession, as in "The MP's expenses claim raised some eyebrows" and "He was hiding in the MPs' bar when the police arrived".

Acronyms are like initialisms except that the letters are not pronounced as separate letters but are used to form a new word, as in NASA and NATO. Some acronyms consist entirely of capital letters, others only have a capital at the beginning. Some acronyms have become words in their own right, and their original form has been forgotten. This is unsurprising when you consider that the original form of the acronym 'laser' is 'light amplification by stimulated emission of radiation' which doesn't exactly trip off the tongue!

And, with that, we have successfully dug out our

foundations and are ready to start building our house. (Please tell me when I've stretched this house-building metaphor to breaking point.)

Our foundations were built from words and words combine to make...

Chapter 13
Phrases

A phrase is a small collection of words which, together, form a unit (which makes sense) within a **clause**. A noun phrase is built around a noun as in "The cat sat down". A verb phrase is, unsurprisingly, built around a verb as in "He was sitting still". An adjective phrase - all together now - is built around an adjective as in "She was very boring". An adverbial phrase is built around... come on, have a guess... yes, an adverb as in "He left as quickly as he could". A prepositional phrase starts with a preposition as in "The cat was under the table".

Words combine to make phrases and phrases combine to make...

Chapter 14
Clauses

Phrases combine to create clauses. A clause is a part of a sentence (or a sentence in its own right) which contains a verb. There are two types of clause: a **main clause** which makes sense by itself and can be a complete sentence in its own right; and a **subordinate clause** which does not make sense by itself and cannot be a sentence in its own right because it depends on a main clause for its meaning. The purpose of a subordinate clause is to provide additional - though non-essential - information.

A main clause on its own is a **simple sentence**. A simple sentence contains one verb. Often, it is made up of a subject, a verb and an object as in "The cat sat on the mat" where 'cat' is the subject, 'sat' is the verb and 'mat' is the object. In addition, there are function words such as the determiner 'the' and the preposition 'on' which help the sentence to make sense.

If you stick two or more main clauses together using connectives as your glue, you create a **compound sentence**. For example, "The cat sat on the mat *and* the cat fell asleep". This has two main clauses - the verbs being 'sat' and 'fell'. As the subject is the same in both clauses, it would be stylistically preferable to replace the second common noun with a pronoun like 'he' so the sentence would read "The cat sat on the mat and he fell asleep".

If you combine a main clause with a subordinate clause, you create a **complex sentence** as in "Feeling tired, the cat sat on the mat" where 'feeling tired' is the subordinate clause offering additional though non-essential information. 'The cat sat on the mat' is the main clause because it makes sense without 'feeling tired', whereas 'feeling tired' does not make sense on its own, it relies on the main clause for its meaning. Subordinate clauses are usually connected to other clauses with commas. You can move a subordinate clause around, even squeezing one into the middle of a main clause, so long as you demarcate its beginning and end with commas as follows: "The cat, feeling tired, sat on the mat".

Subordinate clauses which are connected to main clauses by connective words such as 'which', 'that', 'whose' and 'whom' are called **relative clauses** as in "I brought a bottle of wine which is from New Zealand". In most cases, you can use 'which' and 'that' interchangeably so the above sentence could just as plausibly be "I brought a bottle of wine that is from New Zealand". The Oxford English Dictionary says that it is 'usual' to use 'that' when referring to things rather than people, however.

My advice: trust your ear.

There is one occasion, however, when 'that' should not be used to introduce a relative clause. A **non-restrictive relative clause** contains additional information that is non-essential to the meaning of the sentence. In other words, a non-restrictive relative clause could be omitted without affecting the sentence's meaning. Non-restrictive clauses can be introduced using 'which', 'who', 'whom or 'whose' but not 'that'. Non-restrictive relative clauses are always preceded by a comma for demarcation. For example, "He brought her lunch, which she ate" and "I played football, which is my favourite sport".

Words combine to make phrases and phrases combine to make clauses. What do clauses combine to make...? All together now... clauses make...

Chapter 15
Sentences

A sentence is a group of words that makes sense by itself. In order to make sense, sentences must contain a verb. To be grammatically correct, sentences must also start with a capital letter and end with a full stop.

There are, as we have already learnt, three types of sentence: simple, compound and complex. A simple sentence contains one main clause, as in "The cat sat on the mat". A compound sentence contains two or more main clauses joined with connectives, as in "The cat sat on the mat and the cat fell asleep". A complex sentence contains at least one main clause and at least one subordinate clause, as in "Feeling tired, the cat sat on the mat".

Sentences can perform different functions. Sentences

that make statements (e.g. "It's cold in here.") are called **declarative sentences**. Sentences which ask questions (e.g. "Can you close the window?") are called **interrogative sentences**. Sentences which give commands (e.g. "Close that window.") are called **imperative sentences**. Sentences which exclaim something ("Stop!") are called **exclamative sentences**.

It's perfectly acceptable - for stylistic reasons - to use sentences which are not grammatically correct - in other words, sentences which do not contain a verb. These are called **clipped sentences** because they have been cut short. If in doubt. Avoid. Them. In. Formal. Writing.

*

Let's take stock: we've built solid foundations out of words, having looked at nouns, verbs, adjectives, adverbs, pronouns, connectives, prepositions and determiners. We've built the house up with phrases on the ground floor, clauses on the first floor and sentences on the second floor. We'll fix the roof on shortly by looking at paragraphs and whole texts but first let's consider the mortar we need to ensure our building blocks stick together. Our mortar is made from...

Chapter 16
Punctuation

I call punctuation our mortar because, without it, nothing sticks... the house falls apart because we cannot understand the meaning of our words and sentences. Take this example...

Let's eat, Grandma

Without that vital comma, rather than suggesting to our Grandma that we enjoy a nice meal together, we are in fact advocating cannibalism and matricide...

Let's eat Grandma.

Not convinced? Then take this example as further proof of the important of effective punctuation...

Jack and Jill went up the hill to... you thought I was going to say 'fetch a pail of water', didn't you? Well, that's what the nursery rhyme propagandists would have you believe whereas in reality Jack had matters of a carnal nature on his mind when he took Jill's hand and led her up the hill. He demonstrated his love for Jill in no uncertain terms atop that hill. And Jill was so affected by what Jack did to her that she had a burning desire to express her feelings to Jack in a letter. Jill's letter went like this...

Dear Jack,

I want a man who knows what love is all about. You are generous, kind, thoughtful. People who are not like you admit to being useless and inferior. You have ruined me for other men. I yearn for you. I have no feelings whatsoever when we're apart. I can be forever happy - will you let me be yours?

Jill

Sadly, Jill spent too much time fetching water and not enough time at school learning about punctuation. Whereas her letter clearly expresses her affection for Jack, she did in fact want to tell him to leave her alone because he had deeply offended her. If you re-punctuate her letter - that is to say, retain every word of the letter and retain the order in which the words appear, but alter the punctuation - it can have the opposite meaning...

Dear Jack,

I want a man who knows what love is. All about you are generous, kind, thoughtful people who are not like you. Admit to being useless and inferior. You have ruined me. For other men I yearn. For you I have no feelings whatsoever. When we're apart I can be forever happy. Will you let me be?

Yours
Jill

In conclusion, punctuation, when used incorrectly, can lead to Grandma being eaten and to Jill being trapped in a loveless marriage.

And having established how important punctuation is, let's turn our attention to how to use it...

Let's start with the easy stuff:

Full stops

Full stops are used: to mark the end of a sentence; in some abbreviations; and in website and email addresses.

Commas

Commas are used: to mark a slight break between different parts of a sentence; to make the meaning of a sentence clear by grouping or separating words, phrases, and clauses; in lists; and in direct speech.

The last comma in a list (called the **serial comma**) - which comes before 'and' - is called the Oxford comma and is not used universally. But in lists where some items have several parts connected by 'and', it makes the meaning clearer to use a serial comma, as in this example: "You need to bring a warm coat, shoes and socks, and a hat." Using a serial comma before 'and a hat' makes clear that 'shoes and socks' are to be considered as one item in the list and are a separate item to the 'hat'.

The use of commas in direct speech requires a section all

of its own...

Direct speech is when a speaker's words are quoted exactly as they were spoken. If the direct speech is introduced by information telling you who is speaking then a comma needs to be placed after the introduction and before the direct speech, like follows: *He said, "This is direct speech."* If the explanatory information comes after the direct speech, then the direct speech needs to end with a comma (inside the inverted commas) unless the speech is a question (in which case it should end with a question mark) or an exclamation (in which case it should end with an exclamation mark), like this: *"This is direct speech," he said.* Or *"Is this direct speech?" he asked.* Or *"Great example!" he exclaimed.*

If a line of direct speech is separated by information about who's speaking then there needs to be a comma at the end of the first bit of speech (as above) and another comma at the end of the information, like this: *"This is direct speech," he said, "which is spoken aloud."*

Whilst we're talking about commas and direct speech, let's look at inverted commas (or speech marks, or quotation marks).

Inverted commas

Inverted commas come in two sizes: the single 'here' and the double "here". Which size you use is entirely down to personal preference because either size is acceptable. Whichever you use, stick to it because consistency is important. Single inverted commas are more commonly used in British English and double inverted commas in American English. If quoted text appears within another quote, then use the size you haven't already used, like this: "And then he said, 'I can't go on like this!' which wasn't what I'd expected him to say."

The final piece of punctuation advice pertaining to direct speech is this: you should start a new paragraph each time someone else speaks, like this:

"Is that a sheep?" Molly asked.

"A sheep? Did you say 'a sheep'?" her mother replied. "It's a goose, you fool."

Molly flushed then whispered, "Well they're both white."

Right, back to **commas**...

Commas can be used to separate clauses in a complex sentence, usually separating main and subordinate clauses as described above with the example, "Feeling tired, the cat sat on the mat." Commas are used to demarcate where a subordinate clause begins and ends because, without them, the meaning is unclear. Often, the subordinate clause will provide additional, non-essential information which can be removed from the sentence without affecting the sentence's meaning - they act as asides like this: "I came here via the motorway, which was deserted, because it was the quickest way."

There is another way to use commas to separate off a part of a sentence: to demarcate a person's name like this - "Janet's brother, John, is a solicitor." This use of commas affects the meaning of the sentence. Without them - "Janet's brother John is a solicitor" - it suggests that Janet has more than one brother and so the name of the solicitor has to be specified. But with commas - "Janet's brother, John, is a solicitor" - it suggests that John is Janet's only brother.

A good test of whether or not you've used commas correctly is to replace the commas with brackets or to delete all the words in between the commas to see if the meaning is affected.

Exclamation mark

An exclamation mark is used to show an exclamation (who'd have thought it?), to show that something is to be said loudly or with emphasis, or to show amusement. Recently, an exclamation mark placed within round brackets (!) has come to be used in order to show that something is being said sarcastically or with irony. Exclamation marks tend to be used in informal writing and should be avoided where possible in formal writing.

Question mark

A question mark is used to show that a sentence is a question. That's it, really. It's simple, isn't it?

Bullet points

- Bullet points are often used to separate out important information or quick summaries of a longer text.

- Using bullets helps the audience to find and assimilate key facts quickly.

- There are some rules to bear in mind, however.

- If the text after a bullet point is a full sentence then it should start with a capital letter and end with a full stop.

- if not, it doesn't need either

Ok, that's the simple punctuation out of the way... let's look at complex punctuation and start with the punctuation mark which is the bane of many people's lives: the semi-colon!

Semi-colon

A **semi-colon** is commonly viewed as stronger than a comma but not as strong as a full stop. There is some truth in this but their usage is slightly more complicated than that implies... A semi-colon is used between two equal clauses. I like to think of the semi-colon as a pair of weighing-scales: the clauses on either side of it have to be balanced. The easiest way to ensure correct usage of a semi-colon is to write a compound sentence then replace the connective word with a semi-colon, like this: "The cat sat on the mat and he fell asleep" becomes "The cat sat on the mat; he fell asleep". Both clauses are of equal weight. Both clauses are very closely related and are, therefore, better contained within one sentence rather than two.

Semi-colons are also useful in long lists. They can separate the items in a list where some of the items themselves contain commas and connectives, like this: "You should bring: a warm coat; a hat and scarf; walking boots, thermal socks and crampons; a map, compass and pencil; and a mobile phone."

Note I also used a colon in that sentence... here's more about them...

Colon

The **colon** has three main uses: it can be used to introduce a list as above; it can be used before direct speech, like this - 'The audience cried: "Encore!"'; it can be placed between two main clauses when one clause is a consequence of the other or when one clause explains the other, like this - "I have one piece of advice: use punctuation correctly".

Apostrophes

Apostrophes, more than any other punctuation mark, cause sleepless nights! Those who are unfamiliar with its usage get hot and sweaty at the thought of using one; those who are pedantic about their usage can be seen marching down high streets brandishing marker pens aloft like weapons, ready to do battle with shop signs which dare abuse the humble apostrophe (hence the term 'the grocer's apostrophe' which is used to describe the errant use of the poor apostrophe on shop signs advertising "apple's and pear's").

And yet, in spite of its ability to strike fear into the hearts of illiterates up and down the land, the apostrophe is actually remarkably simple to use. After all, there are only two ways to use it: for possession; and for omission. Let me explain...

Apostrophes for possession

We use an apostrophe to show that something belongs to (or relates to) someone, as in: "John's briefcase" and "Janet's book". Basically, it's easier to say 'Janet's book' than it is to say 'the book of Janet'.

Of course, English is never that simple! So there are some further considerations to bear in mind when using apostrophes for possession. With all singular nouns (and most people's names), you simply add an apostrophe and an 's' (like above with "Janet's book" as well as "the cat's bowl" and "today's weather"). This is also true of people's names that already end in an 's', like James and Charles - contrary to popular belief, it is not "James' pen" or "Charles' phone", but "James's pen" and "Charles's phone" because we pronounce the extra 's' when we say it. Try it. There's a difference between James and James's, isn't there? The only exceptions to this rule are in the case of some place names and company names (such as St Thomas' Hospital), when the word already has an 'es' sound at the end (like 'Hodges' goal' which is a goal belonging to someone called Hodges), whenever you cannot hear the extra 's' (as in 'Connors' penalty'), and for plural nouns that already end in an 's' (for example, 'He went to an all boys' school'). Note that irregular plurals (those that do no end in an 's', like 'sheep' and 'children') concur with the basic rule of adding an apostrophe and an 's', as in 'He was in the children's ward'.

There's one other caveat: we do not use apostrophes to

show possession on **possessive pronouns** - words like 'his' and 'hers', 'ours' and 'yours', and 'theirs' - because these words already show possession; for the same reason, we do not use apostrophes to show possession on **possessive determiners** - words like 'his' and 'her', 'our' and 'your' and 'their' and 'its'.

Speaking of which, it's probably as good a time as any to look a little deeper into the **its** and **it's** rule...

When showing possession - that something belongs to 'it' - you never use an apostrophe. For example, "The cat preened *its* whiskers" and "the government was disappointed with *its* support in parliament".

When *its* is written with an apostrophe (it's), it is always short for 'it is' or 'it has', as in: "It's time for bed" meaning 'It is time for bed' and "It's been years since I saw you" meaning 'It has been years...'.

Apostrophes for omission

The only other use of an apostrophe is to show omission - in other words, to show that some letters or numbers are missing from a word or words. For example, "don't" being short for 'do not', "can't" being short for 'cannot', and "I'll" being short for 'I will'. And also: '90s being short for 1990s.

Apostrophes should <u>never</u> be used to pluralise a word. And when I say *never* I mean *nearly never*... on a very rare occasion it's acceptable to break this rule if it aids clarity as in "Dot all the i's and cross all the t's". Without apostrophes, that last sentence would read "Dot all the is and cross all the ts" and would prove confusing. (As would my earlier passage containing a pro's and con's list.) But, if in any doubt, leave it out!

Hyphens

Hyphens - little dashes like the ones separating this aside from the rest of the sentence - are used, well - in the words of Tommy Cooper - just like that... to separate out a clause when you want to show it is an aside or after-thought, or not essential to understanding the main sentence. Basically, you can use hyphens in place of commas at the beginning and end of a subordinate clause. Technically, these are **dashes** not hyphens, the difference being that dashes are slightly longer than hyphens. But they're usually the same button on a keyboard and some word-processing programmes do not differentiate so neither shall I.

Hyphens are also used to join some words together to form compounds like "father-in-law" and "cold-blooded". Hyphenating words is much less common today than it used to be. They are now only used to avoid confusion or to indicate that the words have a combined meaning. The most common form of hyphenated words is the **compound adjective** which is placed before the subject (as in "The good-looking man" and "The up-to-date accounts"), but not the compound adjective which appears after the subject (as in "The man was good looking" and "The accounts were up to date"). It's also important to use hyphens when indicating age or time, as in "The 2-year-old toddlers were full of energy" because not hyphenating it ("The 2 year old toddlers...") could lead to confusion... is it one 2-year-old or 2 1-year-olds?

Also, hyphens should be used when two nouns combine to make a verb, as in "to roller-skate". But hyphens should not be used when a main verb combines with an adverb or preposition to make a verbal phrase (or phrasal verb), as in "jump down" and "break up". (Don't confuse this with a phrasal verb that makes a noun like "build-up" in "There was a slow build-up of bacteria".)

Finally, hyphens should be used to bolt some prefixes onto words (especially where the prefix ends in a vowel and the word begins with a vowel, as in "co-operation"), to avoid confusion with another word (as in 're-cover' which is different in meaning to 'recover'), and to separate a prefix from a name or date, as in "pre-1990" and "post-Thatcher".

Brackets

There are two types of bracket, [square ones] and (round ones). Round brackets are also called **parentheses** and are used to separate non-essential information from the rest of a sentence (in this sense, they can be used interchangeably with commas and hyphens as described above). Square brackets are used to enclose words inserted by someone other than the original writer or speaker, either to add a comment or to clarify what is being said. (If a sentence starts with a bracket like this one does, it should also end with a bracket, i.e. with the punctuation on the inside of the bracket like this.) If a sentence does not start with a bracket but has a bracket within it then the punctuation should be on the outside (like this one).

So our foundations were built of words, and our main structure of phrases, clauses and sentences. All the bricks were cemented together with the mortar of punctuation. Let's now put all the windows and doors in their jambs by analysing spelling rules and the rules of pluralisation...

Chapter 17
Plurals

We pluralise most nouns by adding an 's' to the end of the word as in cat = cats and dog = dogs. There are, of course, some exceptions to this rule...

- Words that end in a consonant followed by a 'y', like party and baby. For these words, we remove the 'y' and add 'ies'. So 'party' becomes 'parties' and 'baby' becomes 'babies'. Why? Because 'y' is an unusual letter - unique in the alphabet - which can be either a consonant or a vowel. When it acts as a vowel, it makes the same sound as 'i' as in the words 'system' and 'analysis' which sound like 'sis-tem' and 'ana-li-sis'. So, if we simply added an 's' to the end of 'party' or 'baby', the resultant words ('partys' and 'babys') would sound like 'par-tis' and 'bab-is'.

- Words that end in an 's' or letters and combinations of letters that make a sound similar to 's', like -ch, -sh, -x, and -z. If we simply added an 's' to the word 'church', for example, it would become 'churchs' and would sound exactly the same as the singular form. This would naturally lead to confusion. Imagine, for example, asking someone to move some 'boxs' for you... you may well have meant for them to move all ten boxes but because the singular and plural forms sound the same, your lowly servant may have assumed you meant for him to move just one box and left the other nine behind (the fool doesn't even deserve the minimum wage). The exceptions to this exception are words that end in -ch but sound like they end in a -k, as in 'stomach'. Here, you simply add an 's'.

- Words that end in an 'f' or 'fe'. These words always follow the same rule: remove the 'f' and replace it with 'ves'. So 'knife' becomes 'knives' and 'calf' becomes 'calves'. The one exception to this is the word 'roof' which is pluralised as 'roofs'.

- Some words that end in 'o'. Most words ending in 'o' follow the basic rule (solo - solos) and all words that have a vowel before the 'o' follow the basic rule (studio = studios). But some words are excepted from the rule. Here's a list of common nouns ending in 'o' to which you must 'es' to make them into plurals (as in hero = heroes): buffalo, domino, echo, embargo, hero, mosquito, potato, tomato, torpedo, veto. (Source: OED.) And here's a list of words that can be either 'os' or 'oes' (as in halo = 'halos' or 'haloes'): banjo, cargo, flamingo, fresco, ghetto, halo, mango, memento, motto, tornado, volcano.

Chapter 18
Spelling rules

A Capital Idea

The first letter of proper nouns, words which name people and places, as in 'John' and 'London', need to be capital letters and so does the first letter of words that relate to people and places, as in 'Dickensian' and 'British'. Capitals also need to be used at the beginnings of sentences and in titles such as the names of films, books, music and so on, as well as the names of companies and institutions. Every word in a title should begin with a capital letter except for connective words like 'and' and 'but' and 'for'. Headings and sub-headings are different to formal titles: you can either capitalise every word (except connectives) or just capitalise the first word as I have chosen to do.

'i' before 'e' except after 'c' (and on several other occasions)

Need I say more? It's believe but deceive, piece but receipt. The only thing to remember is that the rule only applies to words where 'ie' or 'ei' make an 'ee' sound (so words like 'sufficient' and 'proficient' are excepted, as is 'science'), and even then there are some weird exceptions (like 'weird' in fact). But *'i' before 'e' except after 'c' and when 'ie' or 'ei' are not pronounced 'ee', oh and also in some other situations which you just have to learn* doesn't have the same ring to it, does it? So we can forgive the rule for it's flaws. Besides, the best advice is to follow the rule *'i' before 'e' except after 'c'* whenever you're in doubt and unable to consult a dictionary, but to check the spelling in a dictionary whenever this is possible.

Back to the future

A verb's basic form, as we have already learnt, is called the *infinitive*. The infinitive is changed (inflected) when the verb assumes a tense. The past tense is usually created by adding 'd' or 'ed' to the end of the infinitive, as in 'talk' which becomes 'talked'. The present tense is usually created by adding 'ing' to the end of the infinitive, as in 'walk' which becomes 'walking'. Here are the exceptions to the rule that it's important to know...

- Verbs that end in a silent 'e' like 'smile' lose the silent 'e' before gaining 'ed' or 'ing', as in 'smiled' and 'smiling'. There are some exceptions to this rule, too. Words which would be spelt the same as another word once 'ing' is added (like 'singe' which would become 'singing' if the rule was observed) retain their final 'e' in order to avoid confusion. So 'singe' becomes 'singeing' instead.

- Verbs that end in a vowel then an 'l', like 'instil', have the final 'l' doubled up to become 'instilled' and 'instilling'.

- Verbs that end in a vowel then a consonant and place the emphasis on the final syllable, like 'deter', have the final consonant doubled up to become 'deterred' and 'deterring'.

- Verbs that end with a vowel then a consonant but do not place the emphasis on the final syllable, like 'target', do not need the final consonant to be doubled up and so become 'targeted' and 'targeting'.

 - Verbs that have one syllable and end with a vowel then a consonant, like 'pop', have the final consonant doubled up, as in 'popped' and 'popping'.

- Verbs that end with two vowels then a consonant, like 'peel', do not need the final consonant doubling up, as in 'peeled' and 'peeling'.

 - Verbs that end in a 'c', like panic, need a 'k' adding to the end before applying the suffix 'ed' or 'ing', as in 'panicked' and 'panicking'.

For your -ise only

Words that end with the sound 'eyes' are formed by adding either -ize, -ise, or -yse... so which is which? Well, -ise and -ize are both acceptable in British English (make a personal choice and stick to it: consistency is the only measure of quality!). So you could just as reasonably have 'specialise' and 'specialize', despite what some word processing programmes would have you believe! As you may by now expect, though, there are some exceptions... there's a small number of verbs which must always end in -ise and never -ize. Here's a list of the most common of them from the Oxford English Dictionary: advertise, advise, apprise, chastise, comprise, compromise, despise,devise, disguise, excise, exercise, improvise, incise, prise, promise, revise, supervise, surmise, surprise, televise. There is another set of verbs which, in British English, must always end in -yse. These are (in full): analyse, breathalyse, catalyse, dialyse, electrolyse, hydrolyse, paralyse, psychoanalyse. (Source: OED.) In American English, however, they are always spelt '-yze'.

Words that end in 'our'

In British English, when you add the endings -ous, -ious, -

ary, -ation, -ific, -ize, or -ise to a noun that ends in -our, you need to change the -our to -or. For example, 'labour' becomes 'laborious'. When you add other endings such as 'ful' and 'fully', the 'our' remains unchanged, as in 'colour' which becomes 'colourful' and 'colourfully'.

Words that end in 'y'

When you add a suffix to a word that ends in a consonant then a 'y', you need to remove the final 'y' and replace it with an 'i', as in 'happy' which becomes 'happiness' and 'beauty' which becomes 'beautiful'. The same rule applies when adding an 's' to make the word a plural, and when adding 'ed' and 'ing' when changing the word's tense.

Words that end in 'll'

When adding the suffixes 'ment' or 'ful' and 'fully' to a word that ends in a double 'l' you need to remove the final 'l', as in 'skill' which becomes 'skilful' and 'skilfully'.

Shall I compare thee...?

We have already learnt that adjectives which compare one thing to another are called comparatives (like happier).

Adjectives which compare one thing to everything else are called superlatives (like happiest).

Adjectives are transformed into comparatives and superlatives in a variety of ways dependent on the adjective.

- For adjectives with one syllable - like hot and cold, and big and small - we add 'er' to make them into comparatives and 'est' to make them into superlatives. If the adjective ends in a single consonant then we double-up that consonant. So 'hot' becomes 'hotter', 'cold' becomes 'colder', 'big' becomes 'bigger' and 'small' becomes 'smaller'.

- For adjectives with one syllable which end in an 'e', we add 'r' to make them into comparatives and 'st' to make them into superlatives. So 'large' becomes 'larger' and 'largest'.

- For adjectives with two syllables we add either 'er' or 'est' unless they end in an 'e' in which case we just add 'r' and 'st'.

- For some short adjectives and for all long adjectives with three or more syllables, the word does not change. Instead, we add the words 'more' and 'most' or 'less' and 'least'. For example, 'exciting' becomes 'more exciting' and 'most exciting'.

- For adjectives that end in a 'y', such as happy, we change the 'y' to an 'i' then add 'er' or 'est' ('happier' and 'happiest').

- Finally, there are some anomalies (called irregular comparatives and superlatives) whereby the words are changed entirely, such as: *good* which becomes 'better' and 'best'; and *bad* which becomes 'worse' and 'worst'.

Turning nouns into adjectives and adverbs

To turn a noun into an adjective you simply add the suffix 'ful' and to turn it into an adverb you simply add 'fully', as in 'powerful' and 'powerfully'.

Turning adjectives into adverbs

Most adverbs are made from adjectives with the letters 'ly' affixed to the end, such as 'slowly' and 'quickly'. But - yes, you've guessed it - there are some exceptions. If the adjective has two syllables and ends in a 'y' then you remove the final 'y' and replace it with 'ily', as in 'happily'. If the adjective ends with 'able' or 'ible' then you remove the last 'e' and replace it with 'y', as in 'horribly'.

Those are the main spelling rules to watch out for but there are some other common mistakes and misunderstandings it's worth looking at...

Chapter 19a
Grammar rules I
Common mistakes and misunderstandings...

It's not you, it's I...

People often get confused about which to use, 'I' or 'me'. Many people mistakenly believe that using 'I' (as in 'you and I') is more formal and sounds *posher* and therefore use it in every situation. But 'you and I' is sometimes wrong and 'you and me' is right. Here's how to work it out...

The pronoun 'I' should be used (alongside other subjective pronouns like 'we', 'he', 'she', 'you', and 'they') only when the pronoun 'I' is the subject of a verb. For example, "Janet and I are going for a drink after work". 'I' is the subject of the verb 'to go'. In other words, 'I' is going for a drink with Janet.

The pronoun 'me' should be used (alongside other objective pronouns like 'us', 'him', 'her', 'you', and 'them') only when the pronoun 'me' is the object of a verb. For example, "Grandma stayed with Janet and me". The pronoun 'me' is the object of this sentence not the subject; the subject is 'Grandma'.

If this is confusing, then there is an easier way to remember which to use... simply remove the additional noun (above, remove Janet) and see which makes sense. In the first sentence, remove Janet and try both pronouns to see which is right: is it (a) "I am going for a drink" or (b) "Me am going for a drink"? Clearly, the right pronoun to use is 'I'. In the second sentence, remove Janet and try both pronouns: is it (a) Grandma stayed with I" or (b) "Grandma stayed with me"? Clearly, it is 'me'.

Double trouble

We've all heard a student we're reprimanding insist: "I didn't do nothing". And many of us have replied: "So you admit that you did *something* then?" ...then enjoyed the student's confusion before explaining that s/he used a double negative which makes a positive - if he didn't do *nothing*, he must therefore have done *something*.

A double negative uses two negative words in a single clause in order to express one negative idea but the two negatives act to cancel each other out and therefore produce a positive instead.

But isn't this just plain old pedantry? After all, we all know the intended meaning. "I didn't do nothing" clearly means 'I didn't do anything' *not* 'I did something'. Double negatives are a common feature of spoken English and integral to many English dialects. Double negatives were also standard English before the Sixteen Century. So, in my opinion, we should avoid questioning a student's use of the double negative in spoken language but insist on its removal from formal written language.

To boldly split an infinitive

A split infinitive occurs when an adverb is placed in the middle of 'to' and a verb like the above subheading where I have inserted the adverb 'boldly' between 'to' and the verb 'split' to create the split infinitive "to boldly split". Technically, a split infinitive is grammatically incorrect (because we base our grammar on Latin) and the subheading should read "to split boldly" but this didn't stop the crew of the Enterprise from bolding going where no man had been before, nor did it stop Hamlet from asking 'to be or not to be'. Indeed, sometimes it's better to split an infinitive because it helps convey a precise meaning. Take, for example, the following:

"He really had to watch the replay" suggests that it's important that he watches the replay, whereas

"He had to really watch the replay" suggests that he had to watch the replay very closely.

Five items or ~~less~~ fewer

Grammar pedants tend to shop online these days and have their weekly groceries delivered to their door, not because they are lazy but because they cannot queue at the checkouts without suffering an uncontrollable urge to take out their red pens and correct the 'Five items or less' sign . It's a common mistake to make but here's how to avoid it...

Less is used when you're referring to something that can be counted and/or when referring to a word which isn't inflected when pluralised such as time and money. For example, "If you buy it online you will pay *less money*" and "If you take the by-pass you'll spend *less time* in traffic" and "I prefer the sound of vinyl but records hold *less music* than MP3 players". Less is also used with time or measurements, as in "We're due to be inspected in *less than two years*" and "The hotel is *less than two miles* from here".

Fewer is used when you're referring to people or things in the plural. For example, "I buy fewer CDs these days" and "Fewer than ten people turned up" and, crucially, "Five items or fewer".

Prepositions are not words to end sentences with

As we have already learnt, a preposition is a word which shows a relationship between two things, often where something is in relation to something else. For example, 'up', 'down', 'under', 'over', 'in', 'on' and 'with'. Some people consider it grammatically incorrect to end a sentence with a preposition. For example, instead of writing "I got a big pay-out for the horse I placed a bet on" we should in fact write "I got a big pay-out for the horse on which I placed a bet". And I'd agree that sometimes it sounds better to say "for which" than to end a sentence with "for" but there is no reason why a sentence cannot end with a preposition: it is simple stylistics and nothing more. Often, using "for which" sounds too stuffy and formal and is ungainly to say. Besides, those people who argue that it is grammatically incorrect to end a sentence with a preposition should ask themselves what they're really concerned with.

Kicked in the dangling participles

A participle of a verb gives additional information about

the main clause and is often used to introduce a subordinate clause, as we did above with "Feeling tired, the cat sat on the mat" and "The cat, feeling tired, sat on the mat" whereby 'feeling' is the present participle of the verb 'to feel'. Participles must always be used to describe an action carried out by the subject of the main clause just as it does in our examples above - it is the cat (the subject of the main clause) who is doing the feeling.

A participle must always refer to the subject of the main clause. It must never be disconnected from the subject, if it is it becomes a **dangling participle** because it is left dangling, unconnected, unfinished. For example, "Walking home, the sun started to set". In this sentence, the participle 'walking' does not relate to the subject of the main clause, the 'sun'. Translated literally, this sentence tells us that the sun was walking home. To correct this sentence, we need to introduce the subject as follows: "As I was walking home, the sun started to set" or indeed, "Walking home, I noticed that the sun was starting to set".

There's no 'I' in team (but there is a 'me')

Most people have little difficulty matching their singular and plural words. For example, most people would never dream of saying "I were happy until I mistakenly used a plural verb with a singular pronoun and now I are sorry" nor "We was happy, too, until we used a singular verb with a plural pronoun and now look at the mess we is in".

But many people are confused when it comes to matching collective nouns with verbs. Is it "the team was..." or "the team were..."? Is it "the government was failing" or "the government were failing?" If you worry about this, my advice is simple: get out more. There's far more important things to worry about in the world outside your window than collective nouns. Like Ofsted.

Despite what some people believe, in most cases, there is no right or wrong answer. It is perfectly acceptable to use either a singular or plural verb with collective nouns such as team, government, audience, family, group, committee and so on. So it can be "the whole family are coming round" or "the whole family is coming round". There are two collective nouns which are exceptions to this rule: 'people' and 'police' which should always be used with a plural verb. In other words, it must always be "The people have spoken" and never "The people has spoken" and it must always be "The police have arrived," never "The police has arrived".

Chapter 19b
Grammar rules II
Commonly confused words...

advice or advise?
Advice is a noun; advise is a verb
I'd like to *advise* you against it though I doubt you'll listen to my *advice*.

affect or effect?
Affect is a verb which means 'to change something'; effect is a noun which means 'the result of a change' and 'to make something happen'.

allusion or illusion?
Allusion is to make reference to something; an illusion is an imagined version of the truth.

canvas or canvass?
Canvas is a material painters use; canvass is to ask people for their opinions.

cite, site or sight?
Cite means 'to quote'; site is a place; sight is something you see.

council or counsel?
a council is a group of people elected to make decisions; counsel means 'advice' and is also a name for a lawyer.

curb or kerb?
Curb is to hold something back; a kerb is the edge of a pavement.

desert or dessert?
Desert is an arid place and also means 'to abandon'; dessert is a pudding.

disinterested or uninterested?
Disinterested means 'not taking sides'; uninterested means 'bored'.

have or of?
Though it's a common mistake, the words 'would', 'should' or 'could' are never followed by 'of' (as in could of); they can be followed by 'have'. The confusion arises from the way the contracted version sounds ('could've' sounds like 'could of').

its or it's?
Its means belonging to it; it's is short for it is.

lead or led?
Lead can be pronounced in one of two ways. When it rhymes with 'heed' it means to be in front of something. When it rhymes with 'bed' it means a heavy metal. Led is the past tense of lead (rhyming with 'heed'): "He was led out by the bouncers."

license or licence?
License is a verb; licence is a noun.
Can you license my car for me and put the licence through the letter box.

may or might?
May means things are still possible; might means they are very unlikely.

practise or practice?
Practise is a verb; practice is a noun.
I practise medicine at the local GPs' practice.

stationary or stationery?
Stationary is an adjective meaning 'standing still';
stationery is a collective noun for paper, pens, etc.

their, they're or there?
Their means 'belonging to them'; they're is short for 'they are'; there is a place, often contrasted with here.

were, we're or where
Were is the past tense of 'are'; we're is short for 'we are', and where means 'in what place'.

*

We've built foundations out of words such as nouns, verbs, adjectives, adverbs, pronouns, connectives, prepositions and determiners. We've built the house floor by floor with phrases on the ground floor, clauses on the first floor and sentences on the second floor. We've mortared the bricks with firm punctuation and fitted windows and doors made from good grammar. Now let's fix the roof (while the sun's still shining) by looking at paragraphs and whole texts...

Chapter 20
Paragraphs and texts

In terms of SPaG, it's important to ensure that texts are logically and clearly structured, that they flow naturally. One way to do this is to use markers or signposts at the beginnings of sentences and paragraphs. For example, if setting out a logical argument, it is helpful to signal each new point you make by using words such as the adverbs 'firstly', 'secondly', 'thirdly', and 'finally', as well as phrases like 'on the other hand', and 'in conclusion'. Other useful signposts include: however, in addition to, therefore, moreover, next, then, later, and so on.

Another way to help the reader follow the flow of a text is to use topic sentences at the beginnings of each paragraph. Topic sentences - rather predictably - are sentences which contain the topic. In other words, they state what the paragraph is about.

Of course, the logic and cohesiveness of a text is created in the planning stage as much as it is in the writing stage. A text should always be well-planned (except this book which I've had to write in a bit of a hurry because I have somewhere to be) and a good starting point is to use a mnemonic like APT where:

A = audience

P = purpose

T = technique

Audience

When starting a piece of writing, it is important to consider **who** you are writing for. Is it a young or old audience? A novice or expert audience? Is the audience familiar with English or speaking it as a second language? The answers to all these questions inform the way in which you will write.

Purpose

It's also important to ask yourself **why** are you writing? What is the purpose of the piece of writing you're about to start? Is it to inform? To persuade? To instruct? To entertain?

Technique

In terms of technique, once you're clear on your audience and purpose, you need to consider the language and layout that's most appropriate to the task.

Language

As a starting point, consider the following:

- should it be formal or informal?

- should it be in the first, second or third person?

- should it be in the past, present or future tense?

- should it use short, simple (i.e. monosyllabic) words or longer, more complex/technical ones?

- should it use short, simple sentences by and large, or longer, compound and complex ones?

Layout

Consider which of the following presentational features you should use:

- paragraphs

- columns

- bullet-points or numbered lists

- text boxes

- colours

- pictures and captions

- headings and sub-headings

- different font styles and sizes

During the writing process, it's also advisable to check the following elements of text cohesion:

- **check the flow**: does it make sense, is it easy to follow, is the language consistent throughout?

- **check the relevance**: what is missing that ought to be there, what is present that ought to be omitted, what more needs to be said, is it suitable for the audience?

- **check the paragraphing**: is it in paragraphs, are they of suitable - but varied - length, do paragraphs start logically and with signposts?

- **check the punctuation**: do the sentences make sense, is it easy to read without becoming confused or breathless? Is speech, where relevant, correctly marked out?

- **check the spelling**: if in doubt, leave it out - change the word for one you can spell.

- **check the presentation**: is it legible, is it helpfully and logically set out?

Let's look a little deeper at paragraphing...

If a text is to retain a reader's or listener's attention, it should be varied in its sentence and paragraph structures. It should employ a mixture of simple, compound and complex sentences, and have some short and some longer paragraphs.

Writing in paragraphs has three main advantages:

- it helps the writer think about the text as a whole and about how to divide it

- it helps the writer to think about how their ideas are linked

- it helps the reader carve a path through the text, pausing where relevant and connecting ideas together

- it helps the reader to note where they have read to in the event they need to stop reading until later

*

Another consideration to make regarding text cohesion is the relationship between argument and ornament, thought and its expression. This is especially important when writing to *persuade* because the act of persuasion - according to Aristotle - is brought about through three kinds of proof (pistis) or persuasive appeal: logos (the appeal to reason), pathos (the appeal to emotion) and ethos (the appeal to one's character).

Here are some examples...

Logos

Descartes said "I think; therefore, I am". He was appealing to reason.

Pathos

Antony, addressing the crowd after Caesar's murder in Shakespeare's play, manages to stir the crowd into anger against the conspirators by drawing upon their pity...he does this by calling their attention to each of Caesar's dagger wounds and by combining vivid descriptions with allusions to the betrayal of friendship made by Brutus:

> *Look, in this place ran Cassius' dagger through;*
> *See what a rent the envious Casca made;*
> *Through this the well-beloved Brutus stabb'd,*
> *And as he pluck'd his cursed steel away,*
> *Mark how the blood of Caesar followed it,*
> *As rushing out of doors to be resolv'd*
> *If Brutus so unkindly knock'd or no;*
> *For Brutus, as you know, was Caesar's angel.*
> *Judge, O you gods, how dearly Caesar lov'd him!*
> *This was the most unkindest cut of all*

- from Julius Caesar by William Shakespeare, Act 3, Scene 2, lines 174-183

Antony is, therefore, appealing to the crowd's emotions.

Ethos

In Cicero's speech defending the poet Archias, Cicero begins by referring to his own oratory expertise, something for which he was already famous in Rome. Although, in so doing, he appears to lack modesty, his tactic establishes his ethos because the audience is encouraged to acknowledge that Cicero's public service has lent him a sense of authority with which to speak about another author. In effect, his entire speech is an attempt to increase the respectability of the ethos of literature, largely accomplished by tying it to Cicero's own, already established, public character:

> If there is any natural ability in me, O judges - and I know how slight that is; or if I have any practice as a speaker - and in that line I do not deny that I have some experience; or if I have any method in my oratory, drawn from my study of the liberal sciences, and from that careful training to which I admit that at no part of my life have I ever been disinclined; certainly, of all those qualities, this Aulus Licinius is entitled to be among the first to claim the benefit from me as his peculiar right. For as far as ever my mind can look back upon the space of time that is past, and recall the memory of its earliest youth, tracing my life from that starting-point, I see that Archias was the principal cause of my undertaking, and the principal means of my mastering, those studies. And if this voice of mine, formed by his encouragement and his precepts, has at times been the

instrument of safety to others,
undoubtedly we ought, as far as lies in
our power, to help and save the very man
from whom we have received that gift
which has enabled us to bring help to
many and salvation to some.

- Cicero's 'Speech for Aulus Licinius Archias', translated by C. D. Yonge
(London: Henry G. Bohn, 1856)

Cicero is, therefore, appealing to his own sense of character.

*

Traditionally, oratory - the art of public speaking - was divided into three functions: judicial oratory (forensic); deliberative oratory (legislative); and epideictic oratory (ceremonial or demonstrative). These three branches are also known, rather more simply, as past, present and future.

Forensic: originally, forensic oratory was concerned exclusively with the law courts and used in order to defend or accuse... the judicial orator made arguments about past events and did so with respect of two special topics which Aristotle deemed appropriate for this branch of oratory, the just and the unjust (or right and wrong).

Legislative: legislative oratory was concerned with political speaking. It was centred on policy-making and was thus considered the future because it dealt with the question of whether or not proposed new laws would, if added to the statute book, benefit or harm society.

Epideictic: epideictic oratory was aligned with public occasions which called for speeches to be firmly rooted in the here and now. Funeral orations are a typical example of this. Epideictic speeches often concluded with praise (or indeed blame) and thus has a long history of encomia (language which praises) and invective (language which criticises). Aristotle called this virtue and vice.

Whilst we're sub-dividing and classifying, let us look at how the art of rhetoric can be divided...

Rhetoric as an art has long been split into five main categories or canons: invention; arrangement; style; memory; and delivery. Here's what each means in practice...

Invention: From the Latin meaning 'to find', invention is to do with finding something to say, establishing cause and effect, or comparison.

Arrangement: Arrangement concerns how speech is to be organised. In ancient rhetorics, arrangement referred solely to the defined order which was to be observed in an oration. This order was: 1. Introduction, 2. Statement of facts, 3. Division, 4. Proof, 5. Refutation, and 6.

Conclusions. The introduction was concerned with ethos (establishing one's authority), and the four parts which follow were about logos (employing a logical argument), whereas the final part - the conclusion - was about pathos (employing emotional appeals).

Style: Style is about the artful expression of ideas; whereas invention is concerned with what is said, style is concerned with how it is said. There are five virtues of style: grammar, audience, effective and affective appeals, the guiding principle of decorum, and the importance of figurative speech.

For example, take Julius Caesar's line "Veni, vidi, vici"... Julius Caesar utters a little but says a lot when he declares: "Veni, vidi, vici" which translates as "I came; I saw; I conquered". Speaking with such efficiency is a cunning and knowing ploy because he is talking about a military conquest which has been marked out by the very efficiency of its campaign. Caesar also uses asyndeton (the lack of connective words between clauses) which has the effect of being direct and to the point, once again reflecting his efficient no-nonsense leadership style. Finally, this short line is a perfect tricolon (three parallel clauses of equal length - a least when it is spoken in its original Latin). This mirrors the orderliness of his soldiers as they marched to battle, drums beating out a regular rhythm.

Memory: Memory is concerned with mnemonics which

assist the speaker in learning the speech and help the audience to retain the speech in their memory long afterwards.

Delivery: From the Greek word for delivery, 'hypokrisis', which literally means 'acting', delivery is about how something is said. It is concerned with vocal training and the use of gestures.

In terms of structure, we can learn a lot from the Ancient Greeks about text cohesion...

According to '*The Art of Public Speaking*' by M J Bromley, there are three things to consider when structuring a persuasive text such as a persuasive speech:

> **1. The big idea:** your speech should set out one and only one idea. It has to be big enough to justify speaking about it but your speech must not get clouded or confused by other, less important, ideas or messages.
>
> Your big idea can be exemplified by three points (because three is the magic number). For example, your big idea might be "We have to change the way we work by..." And you might exemplify it by outlining 1. why the way you work now isn't effective, 2. how you want the way you work to change, and 3. what life will be like once you've made the change.
>
> **2. The structure:** how your organise your speech is important because your audience has to be able to follow your argument clearly and logically.

Perhaps the most important consideration when it comes to structure is the overall length of your speech. And the simple answer is this: keep it short! A well-focused, succinct speech is the hallmark of a good public speaker. After all, no one ever complained that the speaker didn't go on for long enough! The only complaints you hear about the length of someone's speech is that it lacked brevity! If that wasn't proof enough, then remember this: Abraham Lincoln's Gettysburg Address was only two minutes' long; Martin Luther King's 'I Have a Dream' speech was, as we've already seen, just sixteen minutes' long. The British pilot Lord Brabazon put it best when he said "if you cannot say what you want to say in twenty minutes, you should go away and write a book about it". And I would honour his twenty-minute marker.

Another structural consideration to make is how to start your speech. The opening lines of a speech have to get the audience's attention, introduce you, the speaker, and provide some sort of overview of what you're going to talk about. Here are some useful 'do's' and 'don'ts' to bear in mind:
- DON'T waste time on pleasantries and apologies: there is no need to tell your audience how delighted you are to be speaking to them today, nor is there the need to say you're sorry you haven't had much time to prepare or that you're feeling nervous. The pleasantries can go unsaid and the mistakes are best left hidden - be confident, assured, positive.
- DO start with a bold statement or fact: say something provocative or pose a controversial question to get your audience thinking. You can qualify it later in your speech: the opening lines are no place to be shy!

Once you've started your speech, the main body of it should be divided into three sections: I always remember what the three sections are by using the mnemonic PEE where each letter stands for...

P = Point. This is an assertion, a statement or declaration which summarises what you think and feel - perhaps it is a policy change;

E = Example. This might be a fact or statistic, or indeed a piece of anecdotal evidence, which supports and exemplifies your point - it provides the reason for a change of policy;

E = Explanation. This is an illustration of your point in practice and must be persuasive if it is to provoke the audience's feelings and thoughts. Explanations might take the form of stories, quotes, visual aids, a physical action or much more besides - but whatever form it takes, it should bring your point - your policy change - to life for the audience.

These three sections can be used in any order. For example, your speech might be structured as EXPLANATION, EXAMPLE, POINT. Here's an illustration...

-start by telling a story which illustrates the big idea in your speech

-then cite the findings of a survey which support the point you're making

-finally, conclude with your big idea.

Here's an example I've invented about film piracy:

"On my way here this morning I was offered a copy of the latest James Bond film - which is still in the cinemas - on DVD for just £5. A recent study by the British Board of Film Directors has found that film piracy is on the increase and is costing the industry millions of pounds every year. It is time to change the law on piracy to bring tougher penalties on those buying - not just selling - pirated films."

The same sections could be shuffled so that the structure is" EXAMPLE, EXPLANATION,

POINT:

"A recent study by the British Board of Film Directors has found that film piracy is on the increase and is costing the industry millions of pounds every year. On my way here this morning I was offered a copy of the latest James Bond film - which is still in the cinemas - on DVD for just £5. It is time to change the law on piracy to bring tougher penalties on those buying - not just selling - pirated films."

Or it could be shuffled to POINT, EXPLANATION, EXAMPLE:

"It is time to change the law on piracy to bring tougher penalties on those buying - not just selling - pirated films. On my way here this morning I was offered a copy of the latest James Bond film - which is still in the cinemas - on DVD for just £5. A recent study by the British Board of Film Directors has found that film piracy is on the increase and is costing the industry millions of pounds every year."

And, finally, here it is in its original form: POINT, EXAMPLE, EXPLANATION:

"It is time to change the law on piracy to bring tougher penalties on those buying - not just selling - pirated films. A recent study by the British Board of Film Directors has found that film piracy is on the increase and is costing the industry millions of pounds every year. On my way here this morning I was offered a copy of the latest James Bond film - which is still in the cinemas - on DVD for just £5."

So, you've started well and have developed your big idea by employing PEE. What about the end? How do you ensure you leave on a high and make a big impression? Here are some 'do's' and

'don'ts':
- DO summarise what you want your audience to do - be explicit about the action they need to take next. Inspire them to act by calling upon the audience values and beliefs again, by reminding them what you and they have in common.
- DO end with a bang: use a device such as a rhetorical question, a quotation or a linguistic device which will stay with your audience once you've left the stage.

And finally on the subject of structure, you need to make sure your speech answers the following questions:
- What? In other words, what's your big idea, product or service? What goal do you want to achieve?
- How? How did you invent your big idea and how does it work in practice? How is it different to other people's ideas?
- Why? Why is your idea important and timely? Why is it needed? And why should other people get involved?

3. The language you use: Strunk and White, in their book 'The Elements of Style', said that speeches "should contain no unnecessary words or sentences, for the same reason that a drawing should have no unnecessary lines and a machine no unnecessary parts. This doesn't mean that you must make all your sentences short or that you avoid all detail. But it does mean that you make every word count".

And with that, we can cast our secateurs aside, peel off our gardening gloves and wipe our brows, satisfied in the knowledge that we've tackled all those spiky thorns (and thorny spikes) and accorded the roses of good grammar enough light and air to flourish.[21]

---

[21] Sorry, I forgot the laboured metaphor warning that time.

PART THREE

The appendices

182

Chapter 21
APPENDIX I
The Key Stage 2 SPaG Tests Explained

The Level 3-5 Test

This test is split into two components:

Component 1 assesses grammar (including Standard English), punctuation and vocabulary, including the following elements of the KS2 programmes of study:

En3.7 Language Structure

a: word classes and the grammatical functions of words, including nouns, verbs, adjectives, adverbs, pronouns, prepositions, conjunctions,

b: the features of different types of sentence, including statements, questions and commands, and how to use them for example, imperatives in commands

c: the grammar of complex sentences, including clauses, phrases and connectives.

En3.6 Standard English

a: how written standard English varies in degrees of formality

b: some of the differences between standard English and non-standard English usage, including subject–verb agreements and use of prepositions.

En3.1 Vocabulary

b: to broaden their vocabulary and use it in inventive ways

d: to proofread – check the draft for spelling and punctuation errors, omissions and repetitions.

En3.3 Punctuation

- to use punctuation marks correctly in their writing, including full stops, question and exclamation marks, commas, inverted commas, and apostrophes to mark possession and omission.

Component 2 assesses spelling, including the following

elements of the KS2 programmes of study:

En3.2 Language strategies

d: proofread – check the draft for spelling and punctuation errors, omissions and repetitions.

En3.4 Spelling strategies

a: to sound out phonemes

b: to analyse words into syllables and other known words

c: to apply knowledge of spelling conventions

d: to use knowledge of common letter strings, visual patterns and analogies

e: to check their spelling

f: to revise and build on their knowledge of words and spelling patterns.

En3.4 Morphology

g: the meaning, use and spelling of common prefixes and suffixes

h: the spelling of words with inflectional endings

i: the relevance of word families, roots and origins of words j: the use of appropriate terminology, including vowel, consonant, homophone and syllable.

The Level 6 Test

This test comprises three components:

Questions which draw solely on the Key Stage 3 programmes of study will often use 'scaffolding', so that they are accessible to Year 6 children working within Level 6. The relevant sections of the Key Stage 3 programme of study that will be covered are as follows:

Sentence grammar

1.1a Being clear, coherent and accurate in spoken and written communication.

1.1c Demonstrating a secure understanding of the conventions of written language, including grammar, spelling and punctuation.

2.3i Pupils should be able to use complex sentences to extend, link and develop ideas.

2.3j Pupils should be able to vary sentence structure for interest, effect and subtleties of meaning.

2.3t Pupils should be able to use the conventions of

186

standard English effectively.

2.3u Pupils should be able to use grammar accurately in a variety of sentence types, including subject-verb agreement and correct and consistent use of tense.

3.4a The study of English should include the principles of sentence grammar.

Standard English

2.3t Pupils should be able to use the conventions of Standard English effectively.

2.3u Pupils should be able to use grammar accurately in a variety of sentence types, including subject-verb agreement and correct and consistent use of tense.

Vocabulary

2.3f Pupils should be able to use imaginative vocabulary.

2.3l Pupils should be able to use formal and impersonal language and concise expression.

Punctuation

1.1c Demonstrating a secure understanding of the conventions of written language, including grammar, spelling and punctuation.

2.3v Pupils should be able to signal sentence structure by the effective use of the full range of punctuation marks to clarify meaning.

Component 1 is an extended piece of writing. The writing is assessed according to three strands, made up of:

Sentence structure and punctuation (SSP);

Text structure and organisation (TSO), and

Appropriacy and vocabulary (AV).

Component 2 assesses grammar, punctuation, and vocabulary, just as at level 3-5.

Component 3 assesses spelling. The format is the same as in the Level 3-5 test but with the addition of words that demonstrate the spelling strategies required for lower-frequency, less familiar words, as per strand 2.3w from the Key Stage 3 programmes of study ("pupils should be able to spell correctly, increasing their knowledge of regular patterns of spelling, word families, roots of words and derivations, including prefixes, suffixes and inflections").

The assessment of these tests employs Bloom's Taxonomy where children's cognitive level is measured on a six-point scale starting with **Knowledge** (example questions: "What is the name of the punctuation mark below?" and "Circle two nouns in this sentence." and "Which word correctly completes the sentence below?"), **Comprehension** (example questions: "Circle the word that describes..." and "Tick the word that means...", **Application** (example questions: "Complete the sentence below with an adjective that makes sense." and "Write a complex sentence using the connective 'because'." and "Which sentence uses inverted commas correctly?", **Analysis** (example questions: "Categorise these into adverbs of time, place and manner." and "Why is a colon used in the sentence below?", **Synthesis** (example questions: "How could the clarity of the following sentence be improved?" and "Re-write it, making changes to punctuation and wording to make it clearer.") and **Evaluation** (example question: "What would be the effect of replacing these parenthetic commas with dashes?")

Children's 'response complexity' is also assessed on a scale which ranges from closed to extended response formats, sub-categorised into a number of types, as follows:

Selected Response which is sub-divided into *Data selection – narrow (DN)* which includes questions like: "Put a tick to show whether each is a main clause or subordinate clause" and "Draw lines to match each sentence with the correct verb", and *Data Selection - wide (DW)* which includes questions like: "Circle the connective in the sentence below."

Constructed response which is sub-divided into *Data transformation (DT) which* includes questions like: "Copy the sentence below" and "Add capital letters where necessary" and "Replace the underlined words with one word of a similar meaning", and *Independent response – within prompt (IP)* which includes questions like: "Insert three missing apostrophes in the passage below" and "Add a subordinate clause to the sentence below..."

Extended response which is sub-divided into *Independent response – strategy defined but no prompt (IU)* which includes questions like: "The word written below has more than one meaning. Write two sentences to show two different meanings", and *Independent response – open, strategy not given (IO)* which includes questions like: "Explain why a comma is needed in the sentence below."

The test questions use the following question stems:

Identify: this assesses children's knowledge of particular terminology, language or punctuation features and vocabulary by requiring them to identify the correct response from a given selection. In most cases, says the STA guidance, "they will have to tick, underline or circle the response". The STA provides the following examples: "Tick one word to complete the sentence below" and "Circle the word/words that..." and "Which sentence uses the [...] correctly?"

Matching: this question stem requires children to indicate their response by drawing a line to pair up two different elements printed on the page, so that children do not need to do any writing writing. Sample questions include: "Draw lines to match each sentence with..."

Complete/correct/rewrite: these questions require children to either complete the target sentence or replace an error within it which is underlined. Sample questions include: "An error is underlined in the sentence below. Write the correction in the box" and "Rewrite the sentence below, changing it to..." and "Copy the sentence below. Add [...] where necessary."

Find/write: these questions require children to generate their own examples of specified language, or to label given language with a technical term. Sample questions include: "Write a complex sentence using [...]"

Explain: these questions require children to express their understanding of particular terminology, language features, and vocabulary by requiring them to analyse and explain, in their own words, how or why that element is used. Sample questions include: "The sentence below has [...] missing. Explain why it needs [...]" and "What is the purpose of [...]? " and "Why is the [...] used in the sentence below?"

The STA guidance provides the following level descriptors:

Level 3

Vocabulary: sequences of sentences extend ideas logically and words are chosen for variety and interest.

Sentence grammar: the basic grammatical structure of sentences is usually correct.

Spelling: spelling is usually accurate, including that of common, polysyllabic words.

Punctuation: punctuation to mark sentences – full stops, capital letters and question marks – is used accurately.

Level 4

Vocabulary: vocabulary choices are often adventurous and words are used for effect.

Sentence grammar: pupils are beginning to use grammatically complex sentences, extending meaning.

Spelling: spelling, including that of polysyllabic words that conform to regular patterns, is generally accurate.

Punctuation: full stops, capital letters and question marks are used correctly, and pupils are beginning to use punctuation within sentences.

Level 5

Vocabulary: vocabulary choices are imaginative and words are used precisely.

Sentence grammar: sentences, including complex ones, and paragraphs are coherent, clear and well developed.

Spelling: words with complex regular patterns are usually spelt correctly.

Punctuation: a range of punctuation, including commas, apostrophes and inverted commas, is usually used accurately.

Level 6

Vocabulary and sentence grammar: pupils experiment with a range of sentence structures and varied vocabulary to create effects.

Spelling: spelling, including that of irregular words, is generally accurate.

Punctuation and structure: a range of punctuation is usually used correctly to clarify meaning, and ideas are organised into well-developed, linked paragraphs.

Chapter 22
APPENDIX II

Commonly mis-spelt words

A
accommodation
actually
alcohol
although
analyse/analysis
argument
assessment
atmosphere
audible
audience
autumn

B
beautiful
beginning
believe

beneath
buried
business

C
caught
chocolate
climb
column
concentration

D
daughter
decide/decision
definite
design
development
diamond
diary
disappear
disappoint

E
embarrass
energy
engagement
enquire
environment
evaluation
evidence
explanation

F
February
fierce
forty
fulfil
furthermore

G
guard

H
happened
health
height

I
imaginary
improvise
industrial
interesting
interrupt
issue

J
jealous

K
knowledge

L
listening
lonely
lovely

M
marriage
material
meanwhile
miscellaneous
mischief
modern
moreover
murmur

N
necessary
nervous

O
original
outrageous

P
performance
permanent
persuade/persuasion
physical
possession
potential
preparation

prioritise
process
proportion
proposition

Q
questionnaire
queue

R
reaction
receive
reference
relief
remember
research
resources

S
sincerely
skilful
soldier
stomach
straight
strategy
strength
success
surely
surprise
survey
safety
Saturday

secondary
separate
sequence
shoulder

T
technique
technology
texture
tomorrow

U
unfortunately

W
Wednesday
weight
weird
women

Chapter 23
APPENDIX III

Subject spelling lists

Art

abstract
easel
kiln
acrylic
exhibition
landscape
charcoal
foreground
palette
collage
frieze
pastel
collection
gallery
perspective
colour

highlight
portrait
crosshatch
illusion
sketch
dimension
impasto
spectrum
display

Design and Technology

aesthetic
hygiene
presentation
brief
ingredient
production
carbohydrate
innovation
protein
component
knife/knives
recipe
design
linen
sew
diet
machine
specification
disassemble
manufacture
technology
evaluation
mineral
tension
fabric
natural
textile
fibre
nutrition
vitamin
flour
polyester
flowchart
portfolio

English

advertise/advertisement
figurative
preposition
alliteration
genre
resolution
apostrophe
grammar
rhyme
atmosphere
imagery
scene
chorus
metaphor
simile
clause
myth
soliloquy

cliché

narrative/narrator
subordinate
comma
onomatopoeia
suffix
comparison
pamphlet
synonym
conjunction
paragraph
tabloid
consonant
personification
vocabulary

dialogue
playwright
vowel
exclamation
plural
expression
prefix

Geography

abroad
function
poverty
amenity
globe
provision
atlas
habitat
region/regional
authority
infrastructure
rural
climate
international
settlement
contour
landscape
situation
country
latitude
tourist/tourism
county
location
transport/transportation
desert
longitude
urban
employment
nation/national
wealth
erosion
physical
weather

estuary
pollution

History

agriculture/agricultural
defence
politics/political
bias
disease
priest
castle
document
propaganda
cathedral
dynasty
Protestant
Catholic
economy/economic(al)
rebel/rebellion
chronology/chronological
emigration
reign
citizen
government
religious
civilisation
immigrant
republic
colony/colonisation
imperial/imperialism
revolt/revolution
conflict
independence
siege
constitution/constitutional
invasion
source

contradict/contradiction
motive
trade
current
parliament
traitor

ICT

binary
hardware
network
byte
icon
output
cable
input
password
cartridge
interactive
preview
CD-ROM
interface
processor
computer
Internet
program
connect/connection
justify
scanner
cursor
keyboard
sensor
data/database
megabyte
server
delete
memory
software
disk
modem
spreadsheet

document
module
virus
electronic
monitor
graphic
multimedia

Library

alphabet/alphabetical
encyclopaedia
novel
anthology
extract
photocopy
article
fantasy
publisher
author
genre
relevant/relevance
catalogue
glossary
romance
classification
index
section
content
irrelevant/irrelevance
series
copyright
librarian
system
dictionary
magazine
thesaurus
editor
non-fiction

Mathematics

addition
estimate
positive
adjacent
equation
quadrilateral
alternate
fraction
questionnaire
angle
graph
radius
amount
guess
ratio
approximately
horizontal
recurring
average
isosceles
reflect/reflection
axis/axes
kilogram
regular/irregular
calculate
kilometre
rhombus
centimetre
litre
rotate/rotation
circumference
measure
square
corresponding

metre
subtraction
co-ordinate
minus
symmetry/symmetrical
decimal
multiply/multiplication
triangle/triangular
degree
parallel/parallelogram
tonne
denominator
negative
vertex/vertices
diameter
numerator
vertical
digit
percentage
volume
divide/division
perimeter
weight
equilateral
perpendicular

Music

choir
minim
score
chord
minor
semibreve
chromatic
musician
synchronise
composition/conductor
octave
syncopation
crotchet
orchestra/orchestral
tempo
dynamics
ostinato
ternary
harmony
percussion
timbre
instrument/instrumental
pitch
triad
interval
quaver
vocal
lyric
rhythm
major
scale

PE

active/activity
injury
qualify
agile/agility
league
relay
athletic/athlete
medicine
squad
bicep
mobile/mobility
tactic
exercise
muscle
tournament
field
personal
triceps
gym/gymnastic
pitch
hamstring
quadriceps

PSHE

able/ability
effort
reality
achieve/achievement
emotion/emotional
relationship
addict/addiction
encourage/encouragement
represent/representative
approve/approval
gender
reward
communication
generous/generosity
sanction
control
involve/involvement
sexism/sexist
dependant/dependency
prefer/preference
stereotype
discipline
pressure
discussion
racism/racist

RE

baptism
Hindu/Hinduism
prophet
Bible/biblical
hymn
religious/religion
Buddhist/Buddhism
immoral/immorality
shrine
burial
Islam
sign
celebrate/celebration
Israel
Sikh/Sikhism
ceremony
Judaism/Jewish
special
Christian
marriage
spirit/spiritual
commandment
miracle
symbol
commitment
moral/morality
synagogue
creation
Muslim
temple
disciple
parable
wedding
faith

pilgrim/pilgrimage
worship
festival
pray/prayer
funeral
prejudice

Science

absorb
exchange
organism
acid
freeze
oxygen
alkaline
frequency
particles
amphibian
friction
predator
apparatus
function
pressure
chemical
growth
reproduce
circulate/circulation
hazard
respire/respiration
combustion
insect
solution
condensation
laboratory
temperature
cycle
liquid
thermometer
digest/digestion
mammal
vertebrate

element
method
vessel
evaporation
nutrient

Chapter 24
The SPaG Book:

The coffee break synopsis

What is grammar?

Grammar is a combination of:

- **Syntax**: the study of sentence structure, an analysis of main and subordinate clauses, of simple, compound and complex sentences, of subjects, verbs and objects, and so on;

- **Morphology**: the study of word structure, an analysis of stem (or root) words, of prefixes and suffixes, inflections for tense, number and person, and so on;

- **Semantics**: the study of meaning, an analysis of the

things, people, and events we refer to when we're talking, as well as how meanings - both literal (denotation) and implied (connotation) - are conveyed, and how words can mask their true meaning (e.g. through the use of euphemism).

What aspects of grammar should be taught in school?

Grammar teaching must include the linguistic structures of <u>words,</u> <u>sentences</u> and whole <u>texts,</u> and must cover:

- the word classes (or parts of speech) and their grammatical functions;

- the structure of phrases and clauses and how they can be combined (by coordination and subordination) to make complex sentences;

- paragraph structure and how to form different types of paragraph;

- the structure of whole texts, including cohesion, and the conventions of openings and conclusions in different types of writing; and

- the use of appropriate grammatical terminology in order to reflect on the meaning and clarity of both spoken and written language.

Why do we need to teach SPaG?

According to the National Literacy Strategy, the only explicit justification for teaching grammar is its contribution to writing skills. Grammar teaching, the theory goes, promotes students' understanding and helps them to know, notice, discuss and explore language features. The quality of students' writing is also affected by their motivation, creativity and insight, all of which may also be improved by grammar teaching. Grammar teaching may also provide a tool for learning other languages.

How should we teach SPaG?

Grammar teaching works best when it is:

✓ placed in context

✓ made relevant to students' writing

✓ made explicit as well as taught through investigations

✓ revisited systematically

✓ taught across the curriculum not confined to English lessons

Why is SPaG important now?

SPaG is now tested at the end of Key Stage 2. The new SPaG tests assess elements of the current English curriculum including:

- sentence grammar (through identification and grammatical accuracy);

- punctuation (through identification and grammatical accuracy);

- vocabulary (through grammatical accuracy); and

- spelling.

SPaG is also part of the assessment criteria of four GCSE subjects: English literature, history, geography, and religious studies, where it accounts for 5% of the final mark. SPaG at GCSE is about:

- accurate spelling;

- effective use of punctuation to ensure clarity and to aid meaning;

- consistently obeying the rules of grammar; and

- effective use of a wide range of specialist (by which is meant 'subject specific') vocabulary.

Isn't SPaG an English teacher's job?

Yes and no. The National Curriculum and Ofsted say all teachers should view themselves as teachers of literacy, regardless of their subject specialism. Also, teaching literacy is *not* the same as teaching English. Literacy is about helping students to access the whole curriculum. Literacy is about helping students to read subject information and helping students to write in order that they can assimilate that information and then demonstrate their learning.

Teaching literacy might take the form of:

✓ displaying key words;

✓ writing three key words for each lesson on the white board at the start of the lesson and reinforcing the meaning and usage of these words throughout the lesson;

✓ giving students the opportunity to say key words out loud, then asking them to write a sentence using the word in context;

✓ giving students the opportunity to repeat a new skill;

✓ providing students with workbooks to record new vocabulary – like a personal subject dictionary;

✓ providing cut-up sentences on a subject-specific topic and asking students to reconstruct them;

✓ analysing the audience, purpose and style of the texts being studied;

✓ providing opportunities for group discussion and debate, reinforcing the rules of effective group talk.

The history of English

English is very, very old and doesn't make much sense. But it's better than French.

The building blocks of English

It's wise to study English in its component parts starting with:

Letters, of which there are 26, 20 consonants, 5 vowels and 'y' which can be either

which make

Phonemes (units of sound) **and morphemes** (units of meaning like prefixes and suffixes)

which make

Words (like nouns, verbs, adjectives and adverbs, connectives, pronouns, determiners, and prepositions)

which make

Phrases

which make

Clauses (a main clause makes sense on its own because it has a verb, a subordinate clause doesn't)

which make

Sentences, of which there are three main types: simple (subject-verb-object), compound (two or more main clauses joined by connective words), and complex (with at least one main and one subordinate clause). And four main functions: declarative (statements), imperative (commands), interrogative (questions), and exclamative (exclaiming something)

which make

Paragraphs, which might helpfully start with an adverb such as 'firstly, and which are instigated each time a new point is made, whenever there's a time shift or for dramatic effect

which make

Texts, like this book which I hope you have enjoyed and found of good use. Thank you for reading it. Happy SPaG-ing.

ABOUT THE AUTHORS

Matilda Rose is a teacher and writer.

You can follow her on Twitter: @between2thorns

*

M. J. Bromley is an education writer and consultant.

You can follow him on Twitter: @mj_bromley

ALSO BY MATILDA ROSE
The Cruellest Month

ALSO BY M J BROMLEY
Leadership for Learning
Ofsted: Thriving Not Surviving
The IQ Myth
The Art of Public Speaking
How to Become a School Leader

Leadership for Learning
A Senior Leader's Handbook

The Blurb

Countless books have been written on the subject of school leadership: some claim to know the philosophy of school leadership; others promise to share the secret of school leadership. Many of these books have value; they contain nuggets of useful information based on detailed research. But most are theoretical; they are not practical. Once read, they are rarely again consulted. As good as they are, school leaders don't turn to them when they need ideas or inspiration.

The ABC of School Improvement is different: it is a practical handbook for busy senior leaders – a book of ideas which you can put into practice, which can be dipped into when help and advice are needed most. The author is different, too: he is not a university professor; he is a senior leader working in schools every day. He has worked at senior leader level in two secondary schools (one a large inner-city school, the other a small rural school) and has managed every aspect of a school's organisation: he has managed the process of school improvement and self-evaluation, the curriculum and timetable, teaching and learning, pastoral care, administration, finance and the site. He has helped schools on the journey towards 'outstanding': one school became a beacon of good practice in teaching and learning; another became the highest achieving comprehensive school in its authority and the fifth most improved school in the country. Along the journey, he's seen examples of good and bad leadership and has learnt valuable lessons from each. This book is a means of sharing those lessons in leadership.

The ABC of School Improvement covers an impressive range of topics and for every chapter to explore the theory of effective school leadership, there's a series of practical resources and ideas which can be put to immediate use.

Available from www.solutionsforschool.co.uk.

Ofsted: Thriving Not Surviving
Under the 2012 Framework

The Blurb

"A practical, hands-on book written in a fluent, friendly style which makes it easy and enjoyable to read. It makes sense of what is a difficult job and cuts through some complex ideas and issues and makes them accessible."

- Assistant Headteacher

"This book is readable and engaging. It manages to draw you in almost immediately and you find yourself reading on and on, appreciating how one can make a difference."

- School Business Manager

'Ofsted: Thriving Not Surviving' is a useful quick-read for all school leaders but is essential reading for leaders who have not yet experienced an inspection under the new framework.

This book provides a practical walk-through of the new inspection process and is full of helpful advice about how to ensure a smooth, successful visit.

It deftly summarises the new framework as well as the changes expected to come into force in September 2012 including 'almost no-notice inspections'.

The book covers: the new framework; what to do before an inspection; what to do during an inspection; what to do after an inspection; the implications of 'almost no-notice' inspections; Ofsted are not the reason we do what we do...

Available from www.solutionsforschool.co.uk.

The IQ Myth:
How To Grow Your Own Intelligence

The Blurb

Alfred Binet invented the IQ test - not as a measure of innate intellect or ability, nor as a number by which someone's capabilities could be determined - but as a way of identifying children who were not profiting from the Paris public school system. Binet, far from believing IQ was a measure of natural-born talent, said that anyone could achieve anything with "practice, training, and above all, method".

Taking these three words - uttered a century ago - as its premise, "The IQ Myth" explores the importance of hard work and practice - rather than innate ability or intellect - in improving one's intelligence. Primarily written for school teachers - though a fascinating book for anyone interested in the science of how we learn - "The IQ Myth" examines the true nature of intelligence and argues that nurture is more important than nature when it comes to realising one's potential.

"The IQ Myth" argues that teachers who 'dumb down' and expect students to make little or no progress get just that in return: 'dumb' students who make little or no progress. However, teachers who set challenging, aspirational targets and push their students to be the best they can be, teachers who create an atmosphere in which students truly believe they can make progress and exceed expectations, get results.

Building on the work of a range of psychologists and social commenters including Alfred Binet, Carol Dweck, Daniel Pink, Malcolm Gladwell, Matthew Syed and Daniel Goleman, this book looks at a range of so-called geniuses (from Thomas Edison to Mozart) and sportspeople (from Michael Jordan to this year's Tour de France winner Bradley Wiggins) and questions the real secret of success and the damaging effect of praise.

Intellectually challenging but written in a friendly, fluent style, this book is a fascinating quick-read for anyone interested in the nature of talent and an essential read for school teachers who want to motivate their students to get better results.

Available from www.solutionsforschool.co.uk.

AUTUS BOOKS
England, UK

First published in 2013

Printed in Great Britain
by Amazon